Investing in Uncertain Times

Building Your Best Portfolio for Risk and Reward

John F. Merrill

Brian J. Merrill

Tanglewood Publishing
Houston, Texas

Library of Congress Cataloging-in-Publication Data

Merrill, John F.
       Investing in Uncertain Times / John F. Merrill &
       Brian J. Merrill
       p. cm.
       Includes index.
       ISBN 978-0-9657131-1-5

       1. Portfolio management. 2. Mutual funds. 3. Investments.
   I.   Title.

1 2 3 4 5 6 7 8 9 0 / 1213141516

ISBN 978-0-9657131-1-5

This publication is designed to provide accurate and authoritative information in regard to the subject matter covered. It is sold with the understanding that the publisher is not engaged in rendering legal, accounting, or other professional service. If legal advice or other expert assistance is required, the services of a competent professional person should be sought.

   -   *From the declaration of principles jointly adopted by a committee of the American Bar Association and a committee of publishers.*

Acknowledgments

This book would not have been possible without a lot of encouragement by many people. Our family, clients and friends were all valuable in so many ways.

Very special thanks go to Chris Costanzo, Pooja Handa, Judy Latour and Alma Ozuna of Tanglewood Wealth Management as well as Braden Merrill. They put in many hours of hard work on the book and its completion would not have been possible without their dedication.

Another special thank you goes to the rest of the wonderful team that we work with at Tanglewood Wealth Management. No one could wish for a better team to work with.

Table of Contents

x

Introduction

The Uncertain Investment Environment

U.S. investors have had much to contend with in recent years including: terrorism here and abroad, a sluggish economy, political gridlock, very poor markets and non-existent returns from savings vehicles. Taken together, they have created an unfavorable and uncertain investment environment.

Terrorism by Islamic extremists on 9/11 as well as in London, Spain and Malaysia has taken many lives and created tremendous anxiety in the West. As a result, we have entered wars in both Iraq and Afghanistan in an attempt to root out the leaders and perpetrators of these terrorist acts. While successful in part, particularly with the elimination of Osama Bin Laden in 2011, western civilian populations still live with the threat that terrorism will strike at any time. This is one defining characteristic of today's uncertainty.

The U.S. economy grew at an average rate of 3.2% from the end of WWII through the end of 1999. From the beginning of 2000 through the end of 2011, our economy has only averaged growth of 1.8%. Of course, the Great Recession from December, 2007 to June, 2009 played a big role as it delivered the largest economic decline since the Great Depression. Yet the unusually slow recovery from the recession has left little doubt that something has fundamentally changed within our economy….and not for better.

Many observers have dubbed this economic softness the "new normal". They suggest that the primary cause is the unwinding of the excess leverage (debt) that had built up in the economy over the prior decades and that this new deleveraging will continue well into the second decade of this century. While having a beneficial impact on inflation, this slow growth reduces employment, wage growth and the government's ability to spend. All of these add different sources of uncertainty.

Along with the buildup of debt, politicians of both parties greatly expanded the so-called entitlement programs including medicare, social security and medicaid. Whereas once these programs were meant to be a safety net for those in need, today they reach every segment of society - even the wealthiest. Increasing these government programs were an easy way to please constituents (and get votes) as the true costs were far in the future when the politicians who passed them would be long out of office.

That game is over. Yesterday's *future* costs are coming home to roost today. There is inadequate funding for all of these programs. Choices will have to be made as to what gets cut and what remains. These are uncomfortable choices for our politicians who are used to handing out not taking back. These very difficult choices are at the heart of the political gridlock that has been building over recent years. For everyone who has incorporated the projected level of today's entitlements into their personal financial planning, this also creates uncertainty.

This is one of the primary issues that the European Union and Eurozone have been struggling with in recent years. In fact, their debt and entitlement issues are even worse than those facing the U.S...today. However, without strong political actions here at home, the austerity measures and social tension that Europe is struggling with today will be ours in just a few short years.

How bad has this period of uncertainty been for investors? First there was a major bear market from March, 2000 through October, 2002 in which the stock averages declined just under 50%. Then there was the real estate bubble and subsequent collapse. Home equity values fell by half between 2000 and 2011. Real Estate Investments Trusts (REITs) posted a devastating 68% decline between February, 2007 and March, 2009.

Next came the commodity bubble which saw surging prices between 2001 and middle of 2008. Commodity indexes fell precipitously in the second half of 2008 and well into 2009. After a brief recovery, they fell again in 2010 and 2011.

Finally, there was the worst bear market decline in stocks since the Great Depression from October, 2007 to March, 2009. It was tied to the financial crisis and the Great Recession. The U.S. stock market as measured by the S&P 500 index fell 57% from high to low. International stock indexes - including emerging markets - fell even more in that very rugged bear market.

What is an Investor to Do?

An investor could easily be tempted to turn away from the markets altogether and find comfort in the perceived safety of cash type investments. Unfortunately, the interest rates offered on savings vehicles (money market accounts, savings, C.D.s, etc.) have been extremely low since the financial crisis. Such low rates of return will not enhance wealth (after inflation and taxes particularly) nor will they provide a reasonable income for retirement. This is a major source of frustration and uncertainty that will only deepen the longer such rates prevail.

As most of the sources of today's uncertain investment environment are long-term in nature, investors need to find an investment path to the future that has the highest probability of success, even if such times continue well into the future.

Stephen Dubner, co-author of bestselling, *Freakonomics*, had this to say on CNBC (7/10/12) "Uncertainty is a killer of everything. It's a confidence killer.... Human beings make very bad decisions under uncertainty. That's the difference between *risk* and *uncertainty*. Guys who can measure risk, can put a number on it, can operate in (their own) best interest. Uncertainty throws us into this primitive state where we make panic choices."

Turning uncertainty into knowable and measurable risk is the focus of this book.

Until the mid-1980s, diversification was considered the key to safe investing. In the second half of the 1980s, the *art* of diversification was turned into the *science* of asset allocation. In other words, what had been a somewhat fuzzy concept of investing evolved into something measureable.

John Merrill, one this book's authors, conducted extensive studies on asset allocation beginning in 1988. The results of those initial studies have been modified only slightly since 1990. *Investing in Uncertain Times* continues to update the results of those studies and zeros in on their outcomes in the uncertain period of 2000-2011. As the reader will find, the results are quite positive and consistent.

Previewing *Investing in Uncertain Times*

This book is laid out in four sections. The first section, Chapter 1, lays out some important basic investment concepts including:

- Wealth Creation vs. Wealth Preservation investing
- The importance of monitoring the whole portfolio
- Definition of terms used throughout the book
- The importance of just a 1% higher rate of return
- The significant difference between volatility and risk in portfolio planning

The second section of this book (Chapters 2-7) describes and evaluates all of the primary asset classes (investment categories). This section also introduces the Historical Risk/Reward Chart in Chapter 6. This is a tool developed by John Merrill over 20 years ago as a way to layout on one page all of the risks and rewards of owning a particular asset class. Chapter 7 compares the risks and rewards of the most important asset classes.

The third section of this book (Chapters 8-12) develops the best portfolios (asset allocations) built from history's most consistent and predictable asset classes. As investors vary in their approach to risk vs. reward, the best portfolio for a Conservative investor will not be the same as that of a more aggressive investor. All four

Model Portfolios developed in Chapter 9 and 10 produced highly gratifying results over both the long-term past and the period of uncertainty since 2000. Chapter 10 walks these portfolios through the ultimate period of uncertainty – the Great Depression – with results far superior to what most people would imagine. Chapter 12 shows how to maximize retirement income utilizing the Model Portfolios - even during periods of high inflation and poor markets.

The final section of this book (Chapter 13-18) demonstrates a variety of ways of putting these Model Portfolios' asset allocations to work. There is a thorough presentation of index fund/ETF strategies. Chapter 15 demonstrates a methodology for selecting superior mutual fund managers (which has worked extremely well over time) and the last chapter thoroughly discusses utilizing a wealth manager to guide the entire process.

Yes, these are uncertain times. Fortunately, investors have rewarding alternatives that are thoroughly analyzed and stress tested in this book. These portfolios have continued to deliver on the promise of wealth preservation and enhancement as well as a relatively high level of retirement income from the Great Depression through the present. They are likely to continue to be solid choices for the future.

Who Should Read This Book?

Investing in Uncertain Times was written for long-term investors. It will have little value for market timers, active traders or speculators.

Investing in Uncertain Times is intended for any investor who is interested in obtaining more knowledge of the investment process and particularly those seeking more predictability and consistency from their investment portfolios.

This book does not address the many related and important concepts that together provide a total financial plan. However, those financial planning issues which have a direct bearing on investment decisions are addressed. For example, this book shows how to calculate the maximum amount of income a retirement portfolio can provide even if worst case market conditions unfold and under various inflation scenarios.

Investing in Uncertain Times attempts to present all of its information in a user-friendly manner for the reader who has had little experience with investments.

Mutual Fund and ETF Focus

Mutual funds have been available to investors since the mid-1920s. In recent years, both individual and institutional investors have increasingly turned to mutual funds and the similar ETFs (Exchange Traded Funds) as their investment medium of choice.

This is partly the result of the many innovations in the buying, selling and holding of mutual funds. Mutual fund marketplaces first pioneered by Charles Schwab & Company, Inc., offer one custodial account for all funds. They typically offer fee-less and paperless trading, money market fund sweep privileges and electronic portfolio services, such as pricing, performance and tax accounting, all of which now allow mutual funds and ETFs to be fully managed by individuals and institutions alike.

The end result: completely diversified portfolios of mutual funds and ETFs. These are often the stocks and bonds of today's portfolios.

For all these reasons, this book will use a mutual fund/ETF focus wherever relevant. It is also the approach that the authors utilize at their firm, Tanglewood Wealth Management. However, most of the principles, concepts and illustrations are equally valid for portfolios of individual stocks and bonds.

Major Points Highlighted Throughout Text

The following symbols are placed in the margin next to major points in the text:

     Key Point   Valuable New Research

Section I

Your
Wealth and Retirement
Portfolio

Overview
of Section I

How one normally builds wealth during their career is very different from how one should preserve wealth and distribute wealth during their retirement years. These differences need to be recognized and employed.

Most investment professionals remain awed throughout their careers by the power of compounding returns. Maybe this is why Benjamin Franklin referred to it as the "eighth wonder of the world."

One aspect of compounding that never ceases to amaze is the magnified difference in wealth created by minuscule changes in rates of return over time. In this section, the impact of increasing rates of return will be taken one step further - to the bottom line. In other words - how does a change in the long-term rate of return of a portfolio increase or decrease the income that the portfolio can provide during retirement?

This section also contains critical definitions of financial terms used throughout this book. These definitions are meant to be straightforward and easy to comprehend.

In addition, this section introduces the term used throughout this book to signify an investor's long-term investments – the *Wealth and Retirement Portfolio*. The importance of viewing all long-term investments as a single unit with singular performance is a critical step in developing a comprehensive approach to investing.

1

Important Fundamental Investment Concepts

Introduction

Many investors confuse Wealth Creation and Wealth Preservation. While the techniques of wealth creation investing may be essential before retirement, wealth preservation investment techniques are critical for most investors later in life.

Many investors spend the majority of their time juggling their various investments in an attempt to gain a short-term advantage. Other investors are completely wrapped up in the attempt to avoid short-term market setbacks. All too often this preoccupation with individual investments or short-term risks ends up sidetracking investors from the big picture, their long-term retirement objectives.

The lessons of this chapter transcend an uncertain investment environment. The basic fundamentals of long-term investing have not been repealed.

> *"A ship in port is safe, but that's not what ships are built for."*
>
> — Grace Murray Hooper, *A Kick in the Seat of the Pants*

Wealth Preservation vs. Wealth Creation

For most investors, the primary mandate in managing their investments is Wealth Preservation. This phrase has been used so often it is almost a cliché, but what does it really mean and how do you achieve it ... particularly in an uncertain investment climate?

It is helpful to contrast Wealth Preservation with Wealth Creation. These are two distinctly different approaches to investing. In the exuberance of the 1990s the lines between the two became muddled. However, in the less rewarding and more volatile markets since 2000, the distinction has become more important.

Wealth Creation Objective

Wealth creation's objective is to amass wealth. The hallmark of almost every wealth creation technique is *concentration*. To build wealth, one must put a large part of their available assets into an investment that can explode in value or actually produce value where none existed before.

Two examples of wealth creation techniques that often work are starting your own business and receiving company stock options. Examples of wealth creation techniques that work less frequently include: commodity, stock or real estate speculation; drilling for oil and gas; or investing in someone else's business venture.

When it comes to wealth creation, *risk* means the chance of permanent loss in value.

- One company – any company – can reach a peak in value and begin to slide backwards due to obsolescence of products, competition, poor management, or even various types of liability claims.
- An oil well can come up dry or be unproductive.

- Speculative stock or commodity positions on margin, or highly leveraged real estate can easily decline enough in value to wipe out your entire investment.

In all these illustrations, wealth is lost that is not recovered. That is the downside or *risk* in wealth creation techniques...significant and permanent loss of capital.

Wealth Preservation's Objective

Wealth preservation's objective is to hold onto existing wealth and enhance it over time. The hallmark of wealth preservation is *diversification*. To hold onto wealth and know that it will grow over time, you must spread your available assets over so many investments that the permanent loss in value of any one or two investments will be more than made up by gains in the rest of the portfolio. When it comes to wealth preservation, risk means *volatility* – not permanent loss – and that is a big difference.

Diversifying investments thoroughly among deep, liquid markets such as the U.S. stock market, developed international markets, the U.S. Treasury and corporate bond markets, gold and broad real estate programs has always guaranteed wealth preservation in this country. Granted, the various stock, bond, and real estate markets have declined in value during bear markets, yet each of these markets has *always* fully recovered and gone on to provide even greater value at some point ahead.

Lessons From The Great Depression

Some people point to the Great Depression era as a major exception. Weren't most people wiped out when they invested broadly within these very same markets?

The answer points out another very important principle of wealth preservation...the impact of debt or leverage on your investments. It is true that many of the participants in the stock and real estate markets were wiped out in the Depression – no matter how broadly they diversified. However, as discussed fully in Chapter 10, this was not because of the markets themselves, but because of the high leverage or margin used to finance those investments.

An unleveraged, broadly diversified portfolio of stocks and bonds actually produced very acceptable returns in the full 8-year market cycle of the Great Depression. However, leverage can turn volatility risk into a real risk of permanent loss.

The Sum is More Important than the Parts

A few years ago, I (John Merrill) had an appointment with a man I will call Mr. Smith. Mr. Smith, 55, had worked at Exxon for many years. A little more than two years before our meeting, Mr. Smith had elected early retirement. He received close to $1,500,000, which he rolled over into an IRA. He had been investing the money himself but was now interested in our money management services. He was currently acting as a consultant and did not plan to retire for about 10 years, at which time he would live off his portfolio.

After a few minutes of getting to know each other, he asked me how we had performed in the prior year. I told him that our firm had a good year, and the average equity account was up over 20%.

He was silent for a moment, and then he came back with, "I beat you guys. I made 26%!" Well, I was impressed, so I asked him what he had invested in. He responded with the names of two Fidelity funds. He was right; I knew they had done well the prior year.

"That's it?" I asked, a little incredulously. "You invested your million and a half dollar portfolio in just two Fidelity funds?"

"Oh, heaven forbid!" he quickly responded. "I had about $50,000 in each."

"Okay," I queried. "Where did you invest the bulk of your portfolio to earn such a good return?"

"No, you don't understand," he said. "Those are my investments. The rest I keep in CDs so it won't be at risk....so it will be safe."

"King's X," I threw out. "The $1,500,000 is your investment portfolio. The 26% return on the small part of it you call your investments is of little importance. What is important is the total return of the entire portfolio. The size of your retirement income is completely dependent on the return you achieve from the *total portfolio.*"

We spent a few minutes reviewing his rollover IRA papers and determined that his total return on his investment portfolio for the prior year was just a little over 5%! That was the past year's actual return and the real contribution to the financial quality of his retirement.

The Hodge-Podge Portfolio

Most investors acquire their individual investments over time in a somewhat seat-of-the-pants fashion: a certificate of deposit (CD) here, a mutual fund there, this municipal bond, that stock and so on.

Many such decisions are based upon what is *convenient* (local bank), what options are *available* (401(k)), what's *promoted* (broker-dealer) or what's *advertised* (mutual funds). Each institution disseminates financial data - but only about the securities held at that institution.

Most investors are more or less like Mr. Smith. They don't look at their entire portfolio. Moreover, they don't <u>plan</u> their entire portfolio. As a result, they tend to follow and fret over the individual moves and short-term performance of each investment. This can easily cause excessive trading and bad decisions, or at the other end of the spectrum, a stagnant portfolio and no decisions at all.

The Big Picture

Do you know what your *entire* portfolio's return was last year...for the past five years...for the past ten years? Even many sophisticated investors do not have an accurate measurement of their total performance. And many investors who think they know how their portfolio is performing are seriously overestimating their overall results. A study by Dalbar, Inc. (Boston) showed that investors, on average, thought their portfolios were providing investment returns several percentage points greater than they actually were.

Do you know what your portfolio is currently worth? Do you have a computer program or ledger that contains a composite of all of your investments on one page? Do you update and evaluate it at least annually - as a portfolio, not a collection of individual investments? If you are like most individuals, you do not.

Your Wealth and Retirement Portfolio

The portfolio referred to here - and throughout the book - is your Wealth and Retirement Portfolio. This is your long-term portfolio, designed to preserve and enhance your wealth and retirement income.

Your Wealth and Retirement Portfolio is made up of your "liquid investments," investments that are easily converted to cash, such as stocks, bonds, mutual funds, ETFs, insurance cash values, and certificates of deposit.

It does not matter whether you own these investments directly or indirectly for portfolio management purposes. Directly owned investments are in your name or that of your spouse. Indirect ownership includes IRAs, company retirement and savings plans, trust accounts (of which you are a direct beneficiary) or any other portfolio assets that are earmarked for your future enjoyment and will be available for your retirement.

 Your Wealth and Retirement Portfolio should be broken into two time periods - before retirement and after retirement. Your "pre-retirement" portfolio should exhibit more growth characteristics than the portfolio you structure to carry you through your retirement years. Withdrawals for income during retirement make your "after retirement" portfolio more susceptible to risk. You should plan on your retirement lasting at least 30 years with today's increased longevity.

Defining Critical Terms

Before going any further, it is important that you have a quick reference to the precise meaning of certain critical terms as used throughout this book.

Definitions

TIME	Short-Term	A period of less than 5 years
	Intermediate-Term	A period of between 5 and 15 years
	Long-Term	A period exceeding 15 years (easily encompassing most wealth building or retirement portfolios)
RISK	Risk	Possibility of, or intensity of, a decline in market value
	Loss	A decline in value that is not recovered
	At Risk	The possibility of falling short of an investment objective

Definitions

		(Continued)
	Volatility	Large random swings in market value
	Fluctuation	Up and down movements in market values that are historically normal for a particular asset or set of assets
	Decline	Downturn in market value from a prior level
	Recovery	The period after a decline in which the market regains its former high value
REWARD	Advance	Upturn in market value from a prior level
	Return	Total Return - Includes all items of gain or loss, plus dividends and interest
	Riskless Rate of Return	The return from 30-day U.S. Treasury bills
	Risk-Adjusted Return	The total return of an investment adjusted by its volatility (standard deviation)
	Reward	A measurement of the return above the riskless rate
	Performance	The risk and reward characteristics of an investment
ASSET CLASSES & POLICIES	Asset Class	Types of investments grouped together because they possess similar investment characteristics (see page 28 for a list of the major asset classes)
	Asset Class Families	Most asset classes can be grouped into four major families - stocks, bonds, tangibles, cash
	Investment Policy	Establishes and maintains a specific weighting for each asset class family as an investment objective
	Asset Allocation Policy	Identifies the weighting for each individual asset class; the policy may require fixed weightings over time or call for a changing mix of asset classes
MISCELLANEOUS	Wealth	Purchasing power

Definitions

	(Continued)
SBBI	<u>Stocks</u>, <u>Bonds</u>, <u>Bills</u> & <u>Inflation Yearbook</u>, Ibbotson Associates, Chicago
Market Capitalization (Cap)	The market cap of a particular stock is its total market value - the number of shares outstanding times the market price of each share
Correlation	The degree with which the advances and declines of two separate investments parallel each other. Highly correlated assets tend to track each other's movements.

CHART 1-1

Just How Important are Rates of Return?

Let's return to my conversation with Mr. Smith, the retiree from Exxon. He wanted an idea of what level of retirement income he could expect from his portfolio. Using Chart A1-1 in the Appendix, we can estimate the income that his retirement portfolio will provide. A portion of this chart is shown below in Chart 1-2.

As pointed out earlier, Mr. Smith's current portfolio experienced a rate of return of close to 5% the year prior to our discussion. If 5% was his average annual return for 40 years into the future (10 years until retirement plus 30 years after retirement). Chart 1-2 indicates that Mr. Smith's income at retirement (beginning in 10 years) would be calculated as 5.2% of his current retirement portfolio. Applied to his $1,500,000 portfolio, this chart indicates that he would be able to take an annual income worth $78,000 - in *today's* dollars - for 30 years ($1,500,000 x 5.2% = $78,000) after he retires fully in 10 years.

How much Retirement Income Will your Current Tax-Sheltered Account Provide?

Years to Retirement	Average Annual Return on Your Investments					
	5%	6%	7%	8%	9%	10%
10	5.2%	6.6%	8.1%	10.1%	12.4%	14.9%

(Inflation-Adjusted, Retirement Income as a Percentage of the Current Balance of Your Tax-Sheltered Retirement Account)

CHART 1-2
(from A1-1 in Appendix)

Note: In order to estimate future income from a portfolio, it is necessary to make certain assumptions:
- Inflation is assumed to be 3.0% per year (both before and after retirement).
- Retirement income will be adjusted annually by the increase in inflation.
- Retirement income will be paid out for 30 years before the investment principal is depleted.
- The long-term rate of return from a portfolio is constant both before and after retirement.   This is obviously an oversimplified assumption.

The point of this chart is to isolate one variable - the average annual rate of return on Mr. Smith's investments - and determine its impact on his retirement income. As we reviewed this chart together, *Mr. Smith was very surprised by the increase in his retirement income that just a one percent change in his average annual rate of return would make.*

In this example, if Mr. Smith's portfolio were to provide an average return of 6%, his retirement income would increase to $99,000 per year in current dollars. A 7% portfolio return provides him $121,500 per year. *This is 50% more retirement income from just a 2% increase in his portfolio rate of return.* **An 8% return provides $151,500 per year, a 9% return provides $186,000 per year - more than** *double* **the retirement income of a 5% return!**

The rewards of better investing are real and significant. Of course, Mr. Smith already knew he could take more risks in order to make higher returns than he had been making, but he had not understood the magnitude of change in his retirement income that comes from such small changes in his total portfolio's rate of return.

Note: Charts A1-1 through A1-6 in the Appendix will help calculate your retirement income from your current investments and from your 401(k) and/or other ongoing retirement contributions.

Which Financial Risk?

As presently constituted, Mr. Smith's portfolio might be thought of as extremely low risk. With a large investment in CDs, 93% of his portfolio is insulated from market declines. However, there is a different kind of risk to which this portfolio is much more exposed. His portfolio is *at risk* of not achieving the return necessary to support his present lifestyle during his retirement. Mr. Smith had suggested to me that his retirement needs would be about $120,000 per year (in today's buying power) at his retirement. For this objective, his current portfolio is highly *at risk* of falling far short of his needs.

Mr. Smith and I discussed changes to his current portfolio that would bring these two risks more into balance. If he could accept more short-term risk (intensity of portfolio declines), he could practically eliminate the risk of not meeting his long-term retirement income needs.

Mr. Smith was becoming motivated to seek a higher rate of return on his Wealth and Retirement Portfolio. Yet he well understood his sensitivity to volatility. Both his fears and needs are disclosed by his concluding comments.

"I want my portfolio as predictable as possible for the long term."

"I want to keep my overall level of risk as low as possible while setting a course to achieve my retirement income objective."

"I want to know the worst that can happen. How would another major bear market like 2007-2009 affect my portfolio and its ability to maintain my income throughout retirement?"

Notice that the goals are specific to Mr. Smith's personal needs. Success is measured in terms of reaching a stated long-term objective while minimizing risks along the way. This is so much more important than the elusive and fuzzy goals that most investors espouse, such as "maximizing my returns" or "beating the market." Either of these illusive goals may incur substantially more risk than an investor is willing to live with for a goal that is not meaningful to his or her own financial circumstances.

 The bottom line is that Mr. Smith wants to preserve his wealth in these uncertain times while still being able to meet his retirement income needs.

Conclusions

The key objectives of this chapter are:

- Understand the purpose for your investments – wealth creation or wealth preservation - and invest accordingly.

- Put it all together. Assemble all of your long-term investments into one Wealth and Retirement Portfolio.

- Understand the significant difference that just a one percent difference in your average annual return will make in your available retirement income.

- Run your own race. Measure the performance of your Wealth and Retirement Portfolio (as one value) against your own established objective.

You Only Have One Investment *Portfolio* with Many Different Slices

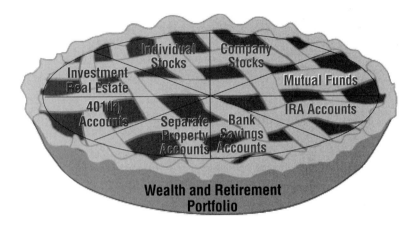

Wealth and Retirement Portfolio

Bottom Line:
It is the performance of the portflolio as a whole that really matters.

Section II

Financial Asset Classes

Overview of
Section II

Are Investment Returns Predictable?

No. Investment returns cannot be forecast with precision either in the short run or long term. However, the *range* of returns that are highly probable becomes smaller and smaller as the time horizon increases. The chart below illustrates this point.

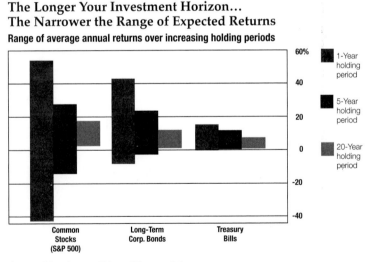

The Longer Your Investment Horizon...
The Narrower the Range of Expected Returns
Range of average annual returns over increasing holding periods

- 1-Year holding period
- 5-Year holding period
- 20-Year holding period

Source: Morningstar Direct, Ibbotson data

One clear message of this chart is that investment returns become more predictable with time. A fundamental premise of this book is that investors with time horizons of 20 years or more should take full advantage of this tendency toward predictability in structuring their portfolios.

Asset Classes

Types of investments with similar characteristics are grouped together as asset classes. As a group, the securities within an asset class tend to react in the same way to economic or investment forces. It is critically important to understand the fundamentals of each of the asset classes available to your portfolio, particularly the degree of risk each takes in order to deliver its return. Your portfolio's mix of asset classes will be far more important in determining its performance than will be your selection of individual securities or mutual funds.

In the broadest sense, there are four families of liquid investable asset classes: common stocks, bonds, tangibles and cash equivalents. The four asset class families are comprised of 12 separate asset classes that will be the focus of this section.

Asset Class Family	Asset Class
Stocks	•Domestic Stocks •International Stocks (Developed Countries) •International Stocks (Emerging Markets)
Bonds	•U.S. Treasury Bonds – Intermediate Maturity •U.S. Treasury Bonds - Long Maturity •Domestic High-Quality Corporate Bonds •Domestic High-Yield (Junk) Bonds •International Bonds
Cash	•U.S. Treasury Bills 30-Day Maturity (equivalent to Money Market Accounts)
Tangibles	•Securitized Real Estate (REITs) •Gold •Commodities

Each asset class has provided the American investor with distinctly different long-term rewards and shorter-term fluctuations. This section of the book will provide a discussion and evaluation of each of these liquid or tradable asset classes with the particular view of long-term inclusion in your Wealth and Retirement Portfolio.

Importance and Availability of Historical Data

Estimating future rates of return is not an exact science. However, without projections of future returns, few people would be able to estimate retirement incomes or the critical spending decisions tied to them. Therefore, it is important to make the most reasonable projections possible.

The history of the financial markets is the place to start. The consistency of long-term, real returns over the past 200 years is the primary basis for confidence in the future. Many financial professionals use the returns shown in Ibbotson's SBBI as a guide to the long-term returns from U.S. stocks and bonds. It provides very accurate index data for major U.S. asset classes back to 1926.

Russell Investments (Russell) developed more "user friendly" indexes in 1982. These indexes for U.S. stocks are more transparent (easily duplicated) and accessible to both institutional and retail investors. In this book, we will use SBBI data through 1981 and Russell data beginning in 1982.

Unfortunately, many other major asset classes do not have this quality of data back that far. We do have quality index data for most of the other major asset classes including international developed stocks, gold and real estate stocks back to 1972 – so that is where our comparisons will begin.

In order to make fully informed investment decisions - particularly in uncertain times - it is insightful to look back at previous periods of uncertainty and the periods that followed.

2

The Impressive Record of Domestic Stocks

Introduction

Stocks, while volatile in the short-term, have been a very rewarding asset class family for U.S. investors over the long term. Events like the 1987 crash, the late 1990s dot com bubble and the 2007-2009 financial crisis lead to the belief that the U.S. stock market is irrational. Yet since 1802, the U.S. stock market has enjoyed remarkably consistent long-term inflation-adjusted returns. U.S. equities are a critical component of the well-designed Wealth and Retirement Portfolio.

> *"The market itself really represents nothing more than a pendulum that swings back and forth through the median line of rationality. It spends very little time at the point of rationality and most of the time on one side or the other."*

> — Robert Kirby, Research Paper at the Institute
> of Chartered Financial Analysts (1976)

The overall poor showing for the broad U.S. stock market since the beginning of 2000 is more the result of extreme overvaluation at the end of the tech and dot.com "bubble" than from poor underlying corporate performance. By early 2012, most of that overvaluation had been worked off and stocks were in a position to be an important driver of future portfolio performance – even as uncertainty continues.

Long-Term Rationality

A basic characteristic of the stock market is that it is both rational and irrational at the same time. The difference is simply the time period under the microscope.

Measured over long periods of time, the returns from common stocks exhibit very rational and rewarding behavior. Essentially, market returns track corporate earnings (profits). For example, the earnings of the stocks that make up the S&P 500 Index were up an average of 6.8% per year from the beginning of 1960 through the end of 2011. The S&P 500 Index itself (before dividends) increased at an average annual rate of 6.1% over that same period. (The total return of the S&P 500 index with dividends reinvested averaged an annual return of 9.4% over that period.) More details on the long-term rewards of domestic stocks begins on page 38.

Short-Term Irrationality

Comparing the performance of the stock market relative to the underlying earnings of its companies over much shorter time periods, however, may show little connection between the two. This is what makes the stock market so frustrating. Earnings often go up while stock prices go down and vice versa.

The short-term fluctuations of any company's stock price is in large part a result of market participants (investors) not knowing what the company's earnings will be ahead. Keep in mind that, while investors know today's earnings, *they* are investing based upon estimates of future earnings.

Estimating corporate valuations is further complicated by interest rates. In theory, the value of a company's stock today is the discounted present value of all future earnings that could be paid out as dividends to the current owner. The discount rate is arbitrary, yet many, if not most market participants believe the best discount rate is the current interest rate for 10-year U.S. Treasury bonds. Therefore, stock prices also reflect changes in interest rates and *anticipated* changes in interest rates...more guesswork.

With all of its uncertainties, frustrations and erratic behavior, market participation draws on investors' emotions. At times, the ever-changing market psychology (the collective enthusiasm or pessimism of participants) goes to extremes. The outlook for future earnings (or interest rates) will reach heights or depths that become very detached from the more probable, mundane reality, meaning stock prices in the shorter term don't necessarily reflect the reality of their underlying earnings potential.

1987 Crash

An extreme example of short-term volatility was provided in one calendar year - 1987. January to August of 1987 experienced an outbreak of market "fever" - one of those occasional periods of over-exuberant market psychology. Market prices as measured by the S&P 500 Index bolted upward by over 23% in just that eight-month period. Meanwhile, corporate earnings were flat to down, and interest rates were rising rapidly (usually a depressant to stock market prices because higher rates cause a heftier discounting of future earnings).

The infamous crash of 1987 occurred in the three months of September through November when stock prices fell over 30% from their August highs.

Unfortunately, this is *not* a singular aberration. Such bull market exuberance followed by a sharp bear market decline has occurred many times over the market's long history. What was new, and very unnerving, was the 22% decline in the Dow Jones Industrial Average in a single day!

The crash of 1987 received a lot more attention than the steep rally that preceded it. In reality, the crash of 1987 was a correction of market psychology as much as it was a correction of market prices. Such corrections have a way of bringing market expectations back to earth.

Note: It is interesting to view the full calendar year of 1987 as one piece of market history. For those 12 months, the S&P 500 index was up 5.2%. Reviewing changing stock prices for the year-as-whole, one might assume that the year was a yawner and that it had exhibited perfectly rational long-term behavior.

2010 Flash Crash

The aptly named "Flash Crash" was an extreme example of intraday volatility. On May 6, 2010, U.S. stocks opened down and trended down most of the day. At 2:42 p.m. (E.S.T.), with the Dow already down 300 points, the market began to fall rapidly – dropping more than 600 points in 5 minutes. Twenty minutes later, by 3:07 p.m., the market regained most of the 600 point free fall.

After months of investigations, the cause of the flash crash was traced to an unusually large sale of S&P 500 futures contracts by a mutual fund company. This trade overwhelmed the market's available buyers which then triggered automated selling from some high frequency traders.

After completing their investigation officials of the S.E.C., N.Y.S.E. and NASDAQ announced new trading curbs and circuit breakers to interrupt a sequence of events like those that caused the flash crash.

Bear Markets, Recoveries and Bull Markets

One way of characterizing longer term stock market (or any asset class) movements is in bull markets and bear markets. A Bear Market is a period of generally falling stock prices. Based on month-end total return data going back to 1950, bear markets for the S&P 500 index have been short (two to three months) or much longer (21-25 months). Bear market declines have ranged from as little as <15%> to as much as <51%> (11/ 2007 to 02/ 2009). There have been three major bear markets since 1950 with declines of over <40%>.

A Recovery is the period following a bear market that returns the stock market to its prior high – before the bear market began (again based upon total return, month-end data). Until the year 2000, each bear market since 1950 for the S&P 500 index had fully recovered within two years. However, the bear market of 9/2000 to 9/2002 took a little over four years to fully recover and the full recovery from the 11/ 2007 to 2/ 2009 bear market has not been determined as of the publishing of this book, although it was extremely close at the end of March, 2012.

A Bull Market is a period of generally rising prices. It includes the recovery period and extends all the way to the beginning of the next bear market. Bull markets have been as short as two years and as long as seven and a half years. Bull market gains have ranged between 63% and 355% for the S&P 500 since 1950.

Bull Market "Bubble"

An irrational bull market occurred in the late 1990's through early 2000. Beginning in 1995, a "normal" bull market mutated into something very different – a bubble. From 1995 through 1999, the S&P 500 Index produced an annualized gain of 25.3% and the NASDAQ surged at an annualized rate of 41.6%!

Just how crazy that bull market became can be judged from some of the valuation metrics used by Wall Street to justify outlandish prices. One such technique was to judge the value of an internet company by the number of logins ("eyeballs") its site registered even if there were no sales – in fact, even if there was nothing to sell! Another technique was to value telecommunication companies by the miles of fiber optics they laid....whether or not there were users for the new fiber!

Even mainstream companies, especially in the technology, telecommunications and media sectors were sold at valuation levels that were far, far above normal toward the end of the "bubble". In order to better understand the extreme overvaluation of the U.S. stock market at the end of the bubble, we will discuss one important measure of stock market valuation – the P/E Ratio.

The Importance of the Market Multiple (P/E Ratio)

What is the market multiple? Why is it important?

The best single expression of the intrinsic value of the stock market is the market multiple. At any point in time, the U.S. stock market - as typically denoted by the S&P 500 Index - is selling at a multiple of the combined per share earnings of the companies that make up that index. [For example, if the S&P 500 index was currently at 1350 and the combined per share earnings of the 500 companies in the index had added up to $100 for the past 12 months, the P/E ratio of the market would be 1350/100 = 13.5. The S&P 500 is selling for 13.5 times earnings or a market multiple of 13.5 in this instance.]

For the past 80 years, the market multiple for the U.S. stock market has *normally* ranged between 10 and 22 times earnings. The average has been about 16. The higher the current market multiple, the rosier the consensus view is about corporate earnings, inflation and interest rates ahead.

But higher-than-average market multiples imply that the market has less room to rise based on the multiple itself going up further. It is less likely that investors are willing to pay still more per one dollar of earnings. It also implies that the market has more room to fall if the market multiple contracts. Conversely, if the market is selling for a lower than normal P/E ratio – as in our example above - it is indicative of a less optimistic consensus view of corporate earnings, inflation and interest rates *looking ahead*. Ironically, a below average market multiple implies a better than average price appreciation in the future should the P/E ratio return to "normal."

P/E Ratio Since 2000

This book was written in 2012 soon after the U.S. stock market had just ended one of the worst 12 year periods in its history (2000-2011). For the entire period, the S&P 500 index's total cumulative return (dividends reinvested) was just 7% (an annualized total return of only 0.5%).

The single biggest culprit for this terrible performance was not political nor was it economic – it was simply the extreme overvaluation of stocks at the beginning of that period. This is clearly demonstrated by the P/E ratio of 37 that the S&P 500 index reached near the beginning of 2000 (the end of the "Bubble"). Not even at the peak of the stock market in 1929 did stock valuations get so stretched. Of course, the cause was the exuberance of the late 1990s tech and telecom bubble.

Over the 2000 to 2012 period, corporate earnings for the S&P 500 companies rose but P/E multiples contracted. By the end of 2011, earnings for those companies nearly doubled from the year 2000 and earnings per share about tripled. However, because the P/E multiple declined to roughly 13 at the end of 2011, share prices were basically flat.

This demonstrates the importance of the P/E multiple for investors. In a period when corporate managements clearly did a good job in growing their earnings, stocks still underperformed as the P/E multiple contracted. Investors paid increasingly less *per dollar of corporate earnings* over this period.

Of course, the good news for investors in early 2012 is that the overvaluation of the early 2000s had been substantially "worked off" and valuation levels were now below average. This will change over time so it is therefore important for investors to always be aware of the current market multiple.

Long-Term Rewards

Despite episodes like the 1987 Crash, the Flash Crash and other bear market periods, domestic stocks have been a very rewarding asset class for U.S. shareholders over the long term. According to Ibbotson's SBBI, from the beginning of 1926 through the end of 2011, the average annual compounded return from the S&P 500 (and its predecessor index) has been 10%. Over that same period, inflation has averaged just 3% annually. Thus, U.S. stockholders have earned the remarkable real return of 7% per year since 1926. This is meaningful wealth creation... doubling the real value of a diversified portfolio of stocks every decade.

Better still, this appears to be the normal, long-term, real return for stocks. Jeremy Siegel, a professor at the University of Pennsylvania's Wharton School, completed an extensive study of the U.S. stock market back to the year 1801 in his book *Stocks for the Long Run* (2008). His major finding: stocks have delivered a relatively consistent $6\frac{1}{2}\%$ to $7\frac{1}{2}\%$ annualized return over inflation in virtually every long period of time (35 years or longer) no matter which year you choose as your starting year for analysis.

The attraction of common stocks is the significant and consistent compounded growth they have historically provided over long periods.

Domestic Advantages

Thus far, only domestic stocks have been discussed. International stocks will be separately addressed in Chapter 4. It is important to note the special advantages that American stocks hold for U.S. investors:

- Currency invisibility – no direct consideration of currency movements or costs

- Ease of purchase and sale (liquidity)

- Wide availability and easy access to markets

- *English* is the de facto business language of the world - but everything is in English here

- Relatively low transaction costs, no transaction taxes.

In addition, the U.S. equity market is by far the largest in the world with over 29% of the market capitalization of equities worldwide. (as of 2011)

Beyond the advantages of U.S. investment markets, there are also cultural advantages that bode especially well for American investment:

- *Incubation of new ideas* – America's fertile intellectual fields are the envy of the world, particularly the depth of our graduate and post-graduate programs. Our universities are the best in the world by far.

- *Entrepreneurship* – The U.S. is unique in small business creation, as well as small business funding through venture capital, initial public offerings, small business loans, etc. Entrepreneurs from around the globe consider the U.S. the best place to launch an innovative new business. No other country in the world comes close to developing great growth companies like the U.S.

- *Technological leadership* – The U.S. has a major or dominant position in almost every industry of the future including: computers, software, telecommunications, biotechnology and the largest proportion of companies with world-class productivity advantages. This technological edge may be expanding. The Internet is overwhelmingly U.S. centric, inundated with English language sites and U.S. generated content. This is the information technology platform of the future.

- *Relatively pro-markets government* – Although far from perfect, the degree of government regulation of markets in America is far less intrusive than most of our major trading partners.

Major U.S. companies dominate many of the important global growth sectors. The U.S. dominates the global technology giants – Apple, Microsoft, IBM, Google, and Intel. It leads in defense technology with leaders like Boeing, Northrop Grumman, Lockheed Martin and General Dynamics. America has almost half of the major global telecommunications companies – including AT&T, Verizon and Sprint.

And U.S. media companies are by far the most prolific globally including the four major networks, plus CNN, CNBC and ESPN. In other words, America is the heart and soul of virtually all cutting edge technology as well as those companies and services that connect the world.

The U.S. is also the home of world-leading industrial companies like GE, 3M, Catepillar and Honeywell and leading energy companies such as Exxon Mobil, Chevron and Halliburton.

The U.S. was rated the top major country in the world for global competitiveness again in 2011 by the World Competitiveness Yearbook (5th overall). Published by the Switzerland-based Institute for Management Development, the study measures and compares the competitiveness of all countries involved in world trade. It defines competitiveness in terms of the mechanisms that help create wealth within a nation. The United States leads in the areas of economic strength, new technology, and in international trade.

In addition, U.S. economic output exceeds that of the two runners - up combined (China and Japan) according to data published by the World Bank. (2011).

While these inherent advantages may diminish in the future, they are very real and significant today and should remain so for many years to come.

In This Age of Uncertainty, Will the Rewards Still be There?

The history of common stocks is richly rewarding, but what is their prospect *going forward?* Will domestic stocks continue to provide long-term returns in the future that are in line with their consistent long-term returns of the past?

Obviously, there are no 100% guarantees, yet the future of the U.S. stock market is tied inevitably to the future of the U.S. economy (and increasingly, the global economy). Both the American economy and stock market have shown remarkable resilience and progress over the past 200 years. From an agrarian economy, through the industrial age, then to the services era and now in the information age, the American workplace has undergone several significant transformations. Yet with all the dislocations caused by these enormous changes - not to mention world wars, cultural revolutions and depressions - there has been amazingly consistent long term economic growth.

Why? People and productivity. The population of the U.S., like the balance of the world, has grown. Each person needs to be fed, clothed and sheltered. The ever larger consumption of an expanding population is a strong driver of growth in the economy.

Productivity is a measure of output per unit of labor. Increased productivity means the economy is getting more production from its labor force, or stated differently, that the economy is growing faster than its workforce. For example, the phenomenal improvements in U.S. farming techniques over the past two centuries is what allows 2% of the current U.S. population to provide all the agricultural products that it took almost 90% of the population to provide 200 years ago. New farm equipment, land management techniques, fertilizers and so forth have produced this miracle.

Productivity encompasses all of the inventions, infrastructure, and increased knowledge that allows the average U.S. factory to put out 60 times as much goods per worker today as it did in 1900. U.S. companies have done a commendable job over time of sharing that growth with both workers and shareholders.

Will the growth in the economy continue? To believe otherwise is to believe that either population or productivity will not continue growing.

Advancements in health and nutrition, as well as the wide global net of their dissemination, are but one reason to expect the population to keep expanding.

As for productivity increases, it is difficult to make any credible case for a slowdown in new developments. There is more money invested in non-military research and development today - by far - than in any other era. If anything, the world seems poised on the edge of major technological breakthroughs in areas like nanotechnology, biotechnology, communications, education, energy, robotics and on and on.

No one knows with any precision what the future will look like. Yet, for investors who own a broad cross-section of U.S. stocks, crystal ball gazing is not necessary. To gain confidence that the long-term upward trend of the U.S. stock market will continue, one only needs to believe that the fundamentals of "people and productivity" are still in place.

Alan Greenspan noted in testimony before Congress (August, 2000) that there is something very special that started developing in the U.S. Economy around 1994 – a dramatic *increase* in productivity. In subsequent testimony through the end of his term in 2006, he reiterated this observation and added that he sees no "credible evidence" that the new higher level of productivity will end. And, in fact, it has continued into the 2010's.

Conclusion

The domestic stock asset class offers long-term investors wonderful benefits. Foremost among these is the significant returns they have provided above inflation over virtually any long-term period. Additional advantages include the breadth and depth of the markets, low transaction costs, currency invisibility and *the* language of business – English. In addition, the U.S. is home to an entrepreneurial culture and maintains a leading position in the industries of the future such as technology, biotech and energy.

While domestic stocks may be volatile and fluctuate irrationally in the short-term, U.S. equities have proved to be the best performing asset classes for the long term. And, as both population and productivity will continue to grow, it is highly likely even with our uncertain future - that domestic stocks will continue to provide rich rewards in the future. Domestic stocks are a critical component of the well designed Wealth and Retirement Portfolio.

Note: The **Russell 3000 Index** is an excellent index of the U.S. Stock Market. The "Dow" and the S&P 500 are more popular indexes but they mainly represent only the largest companies in the country. The Russell 3000 includes 99% of the market capitalization of the entire U.S. stock market. For this reason, the Russell 3000 index will be used to represent domestic stocks when creating asset allocations later in the book.

3

Attractions and Drawbacks of Domestic Cash and Bonds

Introduction

Cash and its equivalents, such as money market accounts, Certificates of Deposit (CDs) and Treasury bills, offer both interest rates that adjust quickly to inflation and a safe haven from fluctuation in principal values. Unfortunately, these assets have also yielded consistently low real returns over any long-term period and in recent years, little return at all.

Bonds typically pay higher yields than cash assets and have produced higher total returns over the long run. Yet bonds are prone to fluctuations in their principal value due to changing levels of interest rates and/or changes in the credit quality of a bond's issuer.

Both cash equivalents and high quality bonds have been an important anchor for portfolios during uncertain times. However, there is a caveat to this general statement when interest rates are extremely low, as they have been from 2010 through early 2012.

"...Diversification is the nearest an investor or business manager can ever come to a free lunch."

- Peter Bernstein, *Against the Gods*

Cash Asset Class

Attractions

Money market accounts are a necessary component of virtually every portfolio. This is the account that transaction proceeds flow through for purchases, sales, contributions and withdrawals. A money market account is an ideal vehicle for parking funds that could be needed in the near future.

While the daily moves in the stock market are often "fast and *curious*," the daily moves in cash equivalent securities ("cash") are monotonously "*low* but sure." One of the main attractions of cash is that you should not find that the investment you made yesterday is down in value today. Only on rare occasions has a money market fund "broken the buck" by allowing its share price to fall below $1.00.

Cash equivalent securities come in many popular forms: money market accounts, certificates of deposit (CDs), commercial paper (short-term notes issued by corporations) and U.S. Treasury bills (T-bills) issued and guaranteed by the U.S. Government.

The return from cash is so nearly certain (little or no fluctuation in the value of principal - up or down) that investors typically accept a very small return over the prevailing inflation rate in exchange for this safety.

On the other hand, this short-term positive is overwhelmed by the long-term negatives of cash equivalents if considered for a major component of your Wealth and Retirement Portfolio.

Drawbacks

Whereas cash is a necessary asset class to hold in some portion within a well-planned Wealth and Retirement Portfolio, it comes with some significant long-term drawbacks:

- Lack of stable or dependable income level,

- Little real return if any (over inflation) and

- Inferior returns relative to stocks and bonds over most long-term periods

An extreme personal example of the first drawback happened in 1981. A fairly young, new retiree (late 50s) came into my (John Merrill) office to discuss his financial plans. He had just received a pension distribution of approximately $300,000, which was all *invested* in a money market account at the then current rate of 16%. He told me that he had retired because he could "make it" on the $48,000 per year that his money market account would pay him. (He assumed the then current 16% rate on money market accounts would last forever!)

This man fell prey to what might be called "current trend tunnel vision"; the feeling that whatever has been happening in the financial markets for a couple of years or more will go on forever. Regrettably, he stuck with his plan, and when interest rates fell from this lofty but temporary perch, he had to find another job.

The second drawback of cash equivalents can be seen in the following chart:

Average Annual Returns

	1926 – 2011	2000 – 2011
Inflation	3.0%	2.5%
Treasury Bills	3.6%	2.3%

Source: Ibbotson SBB1

Chart 3-1

As can be seen in this chart, cash has provided a return of only about a half of one percent over inflation on average since 1926. In the current millennium, since 2000, it has not even kept up with inflation. For the vast majority of people such returns are too inadequate to finance a retirement income.

And the third drawback, the smaller returns from cash vs. stocks or bonds over long periods of time is shown in Chart 3-2. Two long-term periods are illustrated: the full period of SBBI data (1926-2011) and a long-term period that will be developed later in this book (1972-2011).

Average Annual Returns

	1926 – 2011	1972 – 2011
Treasury Bills	3.6%	5.4%
5-Year Treasury Bonds	5.4%	7.8%
Large Company U.S. Stocks	9.8%	9.8%

Source: Ibbotson SBB1

Chart 3-2

Over long time periods – such as a full retirement – the returns from cash have not kept up with those of either stocks or bonds.

Bond Asset Classes

A bond is very similar to the cash equivalent securities such as Treasury bills discussed above but with a longer period until maturity, the date when the principal value of the bond is due "in full." Bonds are segregated in three different ways:

- Domestic or foreign

- Taxable or tax free (municipal) and

- High grade or high yield (junk)

Attractions

The attractions of bonds as a stand-alone asset class are:

- Stable, locked-in rate of income until maturity and
- Typically higher interest rates than cash equivalents.

These attributes of bonds make them an ideal choice for a significant portion of short-term and intermediate-term funding needs (such as college educations) and to match specific financial obligations of a longer-term nature (known pension liabilities for retiring employees would be a good example).

Bonds also offer special diversification attributes when placed within a complete portfolio which includes the lack of correlation of the price movements of bonds with other asset classes. This will be thoroughly discussed in Section III.

Drawbacks

The two drawbacks of bonds as a free-standing asset class are:

- No interest rate adjustments on most bonds during long periods of rising rates, and

- Over most long periods of time, the real returns from bonds have not compared favorably with the real returns of common stocks, particularly after-taxes.

The first drawback was realized in spades by the bond buyers of the 1940s, 1950s and early 1960s. They were never adequately compensated for the rising levels of both inflation and interest rates that began in the mid-1960s. For example, the buyer of a 30-year U.S. Treasury bond in the late 1940s and early 1950s was stuck with an interest rate under 3% for *three decades*, a period in which inflation rose as high as 14% and interest rates on new Treasury bonds reached 15%.

Selling those 3% bonds in the open market along the way would have incurred a huge loss in principal from the original cost while holding on to those bonds incurred a very large "opportunity cost" of not enjoying the higher returns that were to follow.

Warning! In early 2012, as this book is written, the interest rate of new 30-year U.S. Treasury bonds is – like the earlier period after WWII – in the low 3% range. (See Chart 3-3) Could history repeat itself and provide most long-term bond buyers of this era a similar fate? Most definitely!

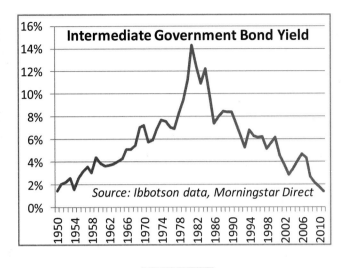

Chart 3-3

The three forces that drove down bond coupon rates to such low yields after W.W.II are the same as in the current period:

- Large government debts to finance

- A Federal Reserve willing to manipulate interest rates to very low levels

- Investors turning to the perceived safety of bonds after major stock market setbacks

From the late 1940s to the early 1960s, it was the post WWII debts that needed financing and the Federal Reserve kept interest rates very low to help accommodate this. In that period, stock investors were still scared by the memory of the Great Depression and the major stock market declines that occurred.

In the current period, the U.S. government (as with most developed countries) has accumulated huge debts in response to the financial crisis and Great Recession of 2007-2009. The Federal Reserve has used both traditional and non-traditional policies to bring near term U.S. treasury rates to near zero and reduce longer term rates to historically low levels. (These low rates minimize the interest or carrying cost of the large government debt for the government).

And, of course, many stock investors in recent years have been scared by the steep declines experienced during the two major bear markets in 2000 – 2002 and 2007 – 2009 ... just as investors were after the Great Depression.

High Quality Bonds

SBBI has provided detailed information back to the beginning of 1926 for three domestic, high-quality bond asset classes:

- *Intermediate-Term U. S. Government Bonds*   U.S. Treasury bonds 5-year constant maturity

- *Long-Term U.S. Government Bonds*   U.S. Treasury bonds 20-year constant maturity

- *Long-Term U.S. Corporate Bonds*   High-grade bonds of domestic issuers with long-term Maturities

Key elements of their long-term results are shown in Chart 3-4 below.

	1926 – 2011 (85 years)			
	Avg Annual Return	# of Years With Loss	Average Loss	Worst Annual Loss
Intermediate-Term U.S Government Bonds	5.4%	9	<1.7%>	<5.1%>
Long-Term U.S Government Bonds	5.7%	22	<3.9%>	<14.9%>
Long-Term U.S. Corporate Bonds	6.1%	17	<3.3%>	<8.1%>

Source: Ibbotson's SBB1   Chart 3-4

Inflation averaged 3.0% in the period 1926 – 2011. Thus each of these bond categories delivered returns that were either just under or just over *double* the rate of inflation for this period. All three compare very favorably to cash (30 day T-bills) which, as shown in Chart 3-2, returned only 0.6% over inflation.

From a risk or downside volatility point of view, intermediate government bonds are a clear winner. They have yielded an average annual return of 5.4% since 1926. This is a real return of 2.4% annualized after subtracting the 3.0% average inflation of that period. This bond category has fewer years with losses and smaller declines when compared with the other two bond categories. Intermediate government bonds offer important advantages – particularly to risk adverse investors.

Both long-term U.S. government bonds and long-term corporate bonds provided higher average returns than intermediate treasury bonds but with substantially higher downside volatility along the way. Yet their higher volatility pales in comparison to that of stocks. When evaluating the "reward for risk taken" (as we will in Chapters 6 and 7), these bonds offer special benefits to balanced portfolios.

Beginning in the early 1970s, deregulation and innovation came to the securities markets. At the same time, interest rates were rising along with the inflation of that era. In combination, there developed strong demand for high quality bonds. This demand could not be met by the traditional bond categories discussed so far.

In response, Wall Street began to securitize or package a variety of safe obligations such as home mortgages, auto loans, and government agency debt. These traditional securitized bonds (unlike the subprime packages of the 2000s) have performed very similarly to long-term corporate bonds. As these offerings provide a wide variety of maturity dates and other flexible features, they have become a stalwart of the bond asset class.

As a result, the composition of the high quality bond asset class has tended to vary over the years based on the rise or fall of the supply of each type of bond. For example, in the late 1990s the "supply" of long-term U.S. government debt diminished when the U.S. budget was in surplus.

In order to capture the entire high quality U.S. bond market ("Total Bond Market"), Barclays and its predecessors have tracked this market with their Aggregate Bond Index. In this way investors can capture the entire U.S. quality bond market or at least have a benchmark for their own bond holdings. This will be the index this book will follow for this asset class.

Treasury Inflation Protected Securities (TIPS)

Treasury Inflation Protected Securities, or TIPS, are a relatively new financial instrument in the United States. Like traditional Treasuries they are issued by the U.S. Treasury and are backed by the full faith and credit of the U.S. Government. However, they have a very unique characteristic – they provide protection against the effects of inflation. TIPS principal and interest payments adjust when there are changes in the Consumer Price Index, (CPI). When CPI rises (periods of inflation), the principal and interest payment increases. When CPI falls (periods of deflation), the principal and interest payment decreases.

Because the principal and interest payments of TIPS adjust with inflation, they help protect the investor's buying power from rising prices. If inflation increases *more than current expectations,* a TIPS holder will be compensated for it. However, the demand for TIPS is based on inflation expectations in the marketplace. These expectations can change quickly, leading to volatility.

Unfortunately, periodic inflation adjustments within TIPS are taxed at ordinary income rates rather than the lower capital gains rate. Taxes are also due every year regardless of the investor's holding period.

TIPS yields are unique in the fixed income world. They are real (adjusted for inflation) yields. Because there is no inflation risk, their yields are usually lower than traditional treasuries. Currently, as this book is written, the real yield from ten year TIPS is actually *negative*! The average yield from TIPS averaged about 1.8% over the prior decade. Investors in TIPS with negative yields will receive *less than* the inflation rate as their total return going forward. Buyer beware! The warning we discussed earlier in this chapter based on the extremely low interest rates on high quality bonds applies to an even greater extent to TIPS with yields below 1%.

High-Yield Bonds

Unreliable History

Most of the available data on high-yield bonds is quite favorable. The problem is reliability. In this case, it is not the reliability of the data. The problem lies in the changing and evolving nature of high-yield bonds themselves.

High-yield bonds are technically defined as those bonds that are rated below investment grade by credit rating agencies, such as Moody's and Standard & Poor's. While this definition has been consistent, the bonds that fall within this definition have changed dramatically over the past two decades. There are four distinct periods in their evolution:

- Before the early 1980s

- Mid-1980s through 1990 (the Michael Milken era)

- 1991-1998

- 1999-Present

The high-yield bond market before the early 1980s was tiny in terms of market capitalization, but the total return on those high-yield bonds was quite favorable compared to U.S. Treasuries - even considering credit risks and defaults. These bonds produced a remarkably consistent default rate of approximately 2% annually but paid a much higher interest rate spread than 2% over U.S. Treasury bonds. Many of the issuers of high-yield bonds in that period were healthy – just small. Often their bonds were not rated because these small companies would not pay the fee required from Moody's or Standard & Poor's to receive a rating.

Michael Milken, a bond trader with Drexel, Burnham and Lambert, took notice of this apparent inefficiency in the high-yield bond market (high returns for *relatively* low risks). Furthermore, he fully recognized its marketing potential. Milken correctly foresaw that more investors would buy these bonds once they were made aware of their risk/reward characteristics.

The problem facing Milken was the tiny size of this market. There was not enough supply of these bonds to satisfy any significant amount of new investor demand. His solution was to generate more high-yield bonds. And that he did. Most of the new high-yield bonds were created to fund the leveraged buy-outs that stormed Wall Street in the 1980s. Unfortunately, these bond issuers had little resemblance to those of the earlier period that had created the attractive track record. The new junk bond issues carried much higher debt ratios and thus were very sensitive to any change in their financial circumstances.

The day of reckoning came in 1989 when the pyramid of leveraged debt (high-yield bonds) began to unwind. Default rates skyrocketed. Worse still, many of these bonds suffered when their collateral was arbitrarily removed in the shuffling of corporate entities that ensued. The high-yield bond market virtually collapsed in 1990.

A new high-yield bond market emerged from the rubble beginning in early 1991. Characterized by super-high yields (demanded by investors) and uncertain collateral, it resembled a flea market more than a securities market.

Uncertainty and Volatility

By the mid-1990s, the high-yield bond market had regained its equilibrium. Important changes occurred in the industry including greatly increased liquidity. In his day, junk-bond trader Michael Milken was the dominant dealer in high-yield securities but was one of the only ones making a market. Orders of $20 million were rare in those days, now they occur regularly.

The quality of new issues improved greatly in the first half of the 1990s. Issuers brought out more senior debt with first call on corporate assets than in the past. However, this asset class is easily abused. In the second half of the '90s, high yield debt was used extensively in financing untested companies (internet startups) and more significantly, the massive over-building of telecommunication networks. Much of this debt eventually defaulted.

Today there are hundreds of dealers, in a sector with about $1.6 trillion in debt outstanding which is about one-fifth of the $7.7 trillion corporate debt market (2011).

The history of high-yield bonds is too short and too erratic to instill confidence in their predictability going forward. Good index data is only available from 1985. Lehman Brothers high-yield index does indicate interesting characteristics for the 1986-2011 time period including higher total returns than other bond asset classes and low correlations with all other stock and bond asset classes. However, it is also much more volatile than most of the high quality bond asset classes. For example, in 2008 high yield bonds *fell* by 26% while intermediate term treasury bonds rose by 13.1% and long-term high quality corporate bonds rose by 8.8%. The reality is that high-yield bonds have more in common with stocks than they do with high quality bonds.

This is an asset class worth watching for consistency and maturity over the years to come. At this stage, however, high-yield bonds appear more appropriate for value investors, traders and other tactical investors to sort through than for those investors seeking a high degree of reliability and long-term predictability from the asset classes they choose for their Wealth and Retirement Portfolios.

Conclusion

Cash is a necessary part of virtually every Wealth and Retirement Portfolio. However, its short-term positives must be carefully weighed with its long-term deficiencies when constructing a portfolio design.

U.S. Treasury bonds of five years to maturity have demonstrated superior risk characteristics when compared to U.S. Treasury bonds and high quality corporate bonds of much longer maturity – slightly less return with much lower volatility.

Both *long-term U.S. treasury bonds and high-quality corporate bonds* have produced higher returns than those of 5-year U.S. Treasuries. Other high quality bond entries – mortgaged backed, asset backed and government agency obligations – have filled out the high quality, U.S. bond universe. They offer attractive risk/reward characteristics that will be explored in Chapter 7.

High-yield bonds are, as yet, too unreliable and too volatile an asset class to include as a permanent position in long-term portfolios where predictability is desired. However, this asset class has ideal characteristics for tactical investors who can correctly evaluate low risk periods for this investment.

 Three of the asset classes discussed - cash, intermediate-term U.S. Treasury bonds and high-quality U.S. bonds ("Total Bonds") - offer many long-term investors attractive benefits for inclusion in their Wealth and Retirement Portfolio.

4

International
Investments

Introduction

Investing internationally entails some thorny issues which must be carefully considered. The most important is that currency gains and losses must be added to the normal investment criteria. This adds a degree of complexity in evaluating international asset classes.

Nevertheless, investing in foreign securities offers some unique advantages as well as a special type of diversification. It is also growing in importance with the rapid development of emerging markets.

In many ways, international investments add to the uncertainty of this era – in other ways, they offer important opportunities to domestic investors.

> *"Globalization has become the financial buzzword of the past decade. The United States, once the unchallenged giant of the capital markets, has become only one of many countries in which investors can accumulate wealth."*
>
> -Jeremy J. Siegel, *Stocks for the Long Run*, 2008

Innocents Abroad

Long known for our parochial, stay-at-home investing habits, Americans in the 1990s burst onto the scene of international investing. One major catalyst was the crash of 1987. Many financial observers noticed that the major international stock indexes did not suffer nearly the decline of the major U.S. stock indexes during the crash.

A second factor was the tearing down of the Berlin Wall and the crumbling of Communism beginning in 1989. The world and all of its stock markets began to appear less menacing, less risky than before. A third impetus to diversifying into international stocks has been the wide circulation of an elliptical curve (developed in the mid-1990s) that showed how Americans could get higher returns with less risk by adding international stocks to their current portfolios (see Chart 4-3 on page 64).

Unfortunately, the reality of international investing in the late 1990s and early 2000s did not live up to the early expectations as U.S. stocks dominated global returns in those years. Yet beginning in 2003, international stocks and bonds – particularly those from emerging markets – began to prove their worth.

Direct international investing has both unique attributes and potential problems which need to be understood and evaluated by the American investor.

International Stocks: Similar But Different

Virtually all of the discussion of domestic stock markets in the first part of Chapter 2 is applicable to international stock markets in that they share these primary characteristics:

- Long-term rationality, short-term irrationality

- Long-term rewards far in excess of their domestic cash and bond markets

In addition, data available on international stock markets for the 20th century (*Triumph of the Optimists*, Dimson, Marsh & Staunton, 2002) indicates similar performance of real, inflation adjusted equity returns between U.S. stocks and international stocks in their own currencies. Whereas the real returns from U.S. equities in this study average 6.7% per year, the real returns from UK, Netherlands, Canada, Australia and Sweden were all between 5.8% and 7.6% annualized. (Germany, France and Japan were much lower - 3.6% to 4.5% - due to the severe impact of the war years.)

This implies that there is universality to stock performance in major markets that cuts across country borders, that business is business in whatever language it is conducted and that the owners of common shares are treated equally in every culture.

There are two reasons why this conclusion is not 100% justified. The first is the limitation of available data and the second is the effect of currencies.

The Lack of Data

CRSP has provided meticulously compiled information on every publicly traded security of operating companies in America back to 1926. (Some of this information is accessed through reference guides like Ibbotson's SBBI.) This allows for in-depth research of every aspect of the risk and rewards of stock ownership in America.

Unfortunately, no such *detailed* long-term database is available for other countries. Therefore, conclusions built on the evaluation of international stocks are somewhat less reliable than with domestic stocks.

 Detailed analysis of international stocks began in 1970, which means that virtually all of the truly in-depth studies of international stocks as an asset class for American investors are conducted in the "new era" of floating currencies.

The Importance of Currencies

International trade and commerce has been conducted for as long as history itself has been recorded. Businessmen want to trade, and no country can produce all the raw materials and finished goods it needs and wants within its own borders. One impediment to international trade has always been the establishment of a common unit of value that both sides could rely upon.

For most of history, gold served as a common currency of equal acceptance in all countries. Any country could participate in world trade if it would declare at what rate its currency was fully convertible to one ounce of pure gold. A gold standard was more or less in effect - with periodic interruptions - until 1971 when President Nixon closed the "gold window" by declaring the U.S. dollar no longer convertible to gold.

From that year forward, most of the major currencies of the world have *floated* against one another with no common anchor for business to rely upon. A change in a foreign currency's value will have the same impact on an American's investment abroad as it does on his/her travel abroad - a direct and immediate impact on cost and value.

The Currency Effect

Investors considering direct investment in mutual funds or ETFs investing in international stocks will have an extra element to their returns and an extra element to their risks. She will have all the risks and rewards of underlying international stocks and additionally have the risks and rewards brought about by the changes in currency values as the foreign market's currencies are converted back into U.S. dollars.

One primary index of international stocks for U.S. investors is Morgan Stanley's EAFE Index (Europe, Australia and Far East). Chart 4-1 illustrates the performance of both the EAFE Index - *in U.S. dollars* - and the S&P 500 Index from the beginning of 1972 through the end of 2011.

For the entire period, the S&P 500 index delivered a 9.8% annualized total return, while the EAFE index produced an annualized 9.0% return for the American investor.

Chart 4-2 also compares the EAFE Index to the S&P 500, but this chart compares *only* the returns from the stocks themselves; the EAFE Index is shown in local currencies - *not* converted into U.S. dollars.

As Chart 4-2 illustrates, the portfolio of international stocks (in local currencies) substantially underperformed the S&P 500 stock index producing a return of just 7.2% annualized for the period.

International stocks substantially underperformed U.S. stocks, but international currencies substantially outperformed the U.S. dollar. You made less on your *investment* in international stocks - but if your portfolio did not hedge your currency risk - you made money on your *currency speculation*!

With perfect hindsight, the big winner of the 1972-2011 period maintained a 100% U.S. stock portfolio (to achieve the better stock returns) and purchased futures contracts on the international currencies, which outperformed the U.S. dollar during the post-gold-standard period.

Brief History of U.S. Dollar (Post World War II)

Before going further, a brief look at why the gold standard fell apart will be helpful in understanding the miserable performance of the U.S. dollar after 1971. The post-World War II gold standard was arrived at by establishing the price of gold at $35 per ounce in U.S. dollars and then pegging other countries' currencies to the U.S. dollar. The U.S. dollar would become the reserve currency of the world, de facto gold.

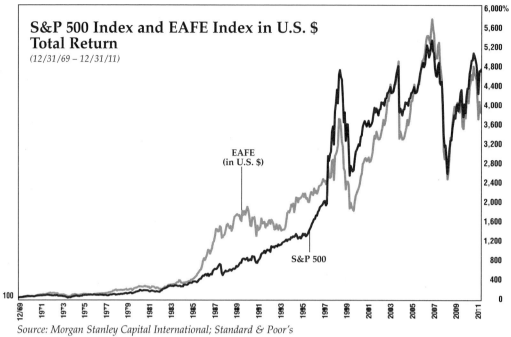

Source: Morgan Stanley Capital International; Standard & Poor's

CHART 4-1

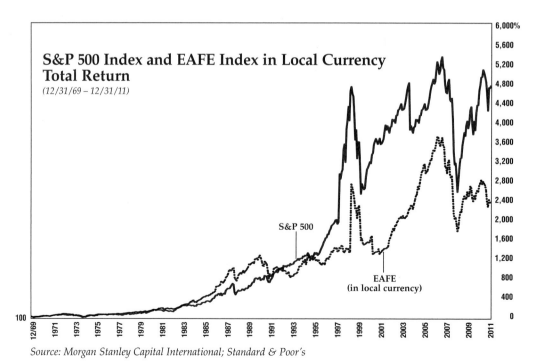

Source: Morgan Stanley Capital International; Standard & Poor's

CHART 4-2

This was the Bretton Woods Agreement that provided the post-WW II world with a stable means of exchange to allow for the massive reconstruction that was desperately needed. Unfortunately, the inflation pressures that would normally be reflected in the price of gold were shifted to the U.S. dollar - because of gold's fixed price (by government decree).

For its part, the U.S. exacerbated the problem in the 1960s by financing both the Vietnam War and the Great Society social programs with printing press dollars, not increased taxes. Other countries recognized that U.S. gold reserves were increasingly inadequate to maintain convertibility to gold at $35 per ounce because of the expanding supply of U.S. dollars. These countries began shipping inflated U.S. dollars back to the U.S. to redeem them for gold. It was the dramatic call on the U.S.'s gold supply and the inability to maintain the conversion that finally "forced" the closing of the gold window by President Nixon.

In other words, by 1971, the U.S. dollar was vastly overvalued at $35 per ounce of gold or conversely, gold was very undervalued at that price. If the member nations to the Bretton Woods could have agreed upon a devaluation of the U.S. dollar, allowing for the convertibility at some higher number like $70 per ounce or more, then perhaps the fixed system of exchange could have survived. (Of course, a method of controlling the U.S. printing press would also have been needed, but this would have meant giving up complete control with regard to internal monetary policy.)

This is an oversimplified view of the maze of post-World War II events, policies and actions that influenced world currencies. What this history provides is a context for understanding the long devaluation of the U.S. dollar that occurred after 1971. From 1971 through 1995, the U.S. dollar lost approximately 75% of its value versus the Japanese yen, Swiss franc and German mark. From 1995 through 2002, the U.S. dollar rebounded sharply – regaining about a third of its prior loss. However, from 2003 through 2011 the dollar more or less steadily lost ground against major currencies.

No Free Lunch

Many proponents of international investing ignore or downplay the role of currencies. As mentioned at the beginning of this chapter, they package international stocks as a *free lunch* for Americans - higher returns with lower risks. Chart 4-3 is a common illustration they use to support their argument.

This chart shows that adding international stocks to a U.S. stock portfolio both lowered volatility and increased returns. When projecting the *future* risks and rewards of international stocks, this chart sends the wrong message. It is based on a unique period of world history in which currencies were removed from the gold standard and the U.S. dollar undertook a long unwinding of excessive valuation. The so-called free lunch was from the weakening U.S. dollar (or strengthening foreign currencies), *not* from international stocks.

In the years after the dissemination of this chart (1995-2002), a large part of the so-called free lunch was given back! During those years, the strength of the U.S. dollar *reduced* the returns from international securities to a U.S. investor. It appears that there will be multi-year periods where the "currency effect" is positive and others where it is negative.

Hypothetical U.S./International Equity Diversification Chart

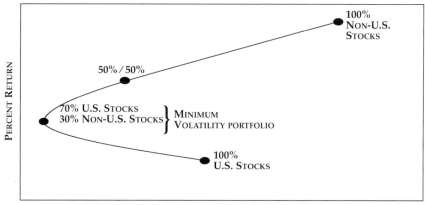

CHART 4-3

In addition, separating the performance of a country's stock market and currency may be misleading. Many economists believe that a devaluation of a country's currency will often make the businesses within that country more competitive internationally and thus benefit local share prices. *This means that you cannot simply strip away the currency effect to get at the real performance of the underlying stocks - one directly impacts the other!*

The Advantage of International Stocks

There is one very powerful advantage to investing in foreign equities: diversification. According to Jeremy Siegel's *Stocks for the Long Run* (2008), "International investing allows you to diversify your portfolio more completely, and it therefore reduces total portfolio risk."

Siegel elaborated on the diversifying impact of foreign stocks in a conversation with John Merrill. He concluded that the long-term expected returns from unhedged foreign equities are about the same from U.S. stocks.

As he expects the returns from foreign equities to remain uncorrelated with U.S. equities over long periods of time, combining U.S. and international stocks will be particularly worthwhile in reducing the volatility of a U.S.-only stock portfolio. In his view, "global investment is best viewed as an extension of domestic diversification." (The impact of foreign stocks within a portfolio will be demonstrated in Section III.)

Emerging Markets

Emerging markets are a new and credible asset class within international investing. Emerging markets are those countries with stock markets that are not considered mature or developed. They may be roughly grouped into four geographic areas: Asia, Latin America, Central Europe/Russia, and Africa.

Can a fundamental case be made for dedicating a portion of a U.S. investor's stock portfolio to these stocks? When this asset class first became popular in the early 1990s, the well-publicized draw was simply, *that's where the growth was!*

Fueled by cheap labor and varying country or regional-specific advantages, the economies of many emerging countries were growing much faster than the 2–3% growth pace of developed economies like the U.S. With such high growth in these economies, their companies and stock markets must outperform those of the more sluggishly growing developed countries, right?

Wrong! Emerging stock markets overheated in 1993 and – led by Mexico – suffered huge declines in 1994. The underperformance continued in 1995 and 1996 and then in 1997 the Asian emerging markets suffered major declines in both currency and stock valuations as investors withdrew their investments. It took years for emerging markets to recover from these losses.

The nature of emerging markets appears to be one of boom and bust cycles. When emerging markets boom, they explode to the upside. The dizzyingly high returns so easy to achieve during these periods are hard to ignore. From mid-1992 through the end of 1993 was such a period. From 2003 through mid-2008 was another.

However, in these two cases, as with most such experiences, after the boom comes the bust. The bottom line is that this asset class has been especially volatile for investors.

Yet despite these booms and busts, the overall average return of Morgan Stanley's Emerging Market Index from its inception in 1988 through the end of 2011 was 11% per anum. Over that same time period, the return from the S&P 500 index averaged 9.5% annually.

In addition, the rising importance and maturity of emerging markets cannot be denied. At the beginning of 2012, emerging markets had these characteristics:

- 86% of the world population

- 50% of the global economy

- 15% of global stock market valuation

When selecting an index to track the international stock markets, the most representative index is the **FTSE All World Ex-US Index**. The more popular MSCI EAFE (Europe, Australia and Far East) index mainly tracks the performance of developed stock markets around the world, leaving out a significant portion of the emerging markets. While the EAFE index was the preferred index for international investing before emerging markets reached size and credibility, the FTSE index is more comprehensive and the preferred benchmark.

Global Investing from the Safety of Home

Investing internationally has become synonymous with investing in foreign-based corporations. It is not the only way to invest overseas, and may not be the safest way.

In all the years before 2000, renowned investor Warren Buffett made but one investment in a foreign company (Guinness, English beverage company). In this case, *he* made the decision to invest internationally. On the other hand, when he made the most significant investment decision of his career (Coca Cola, U.S. beverage company), Buffett in effect yielded to Coke's management the decision to invest internationally.

Actually, both Coca Cola and Guinness are *global companies*. Guinness transacts a significant share of its business in America. And Coca Cola may call America home, yet consider these calendar year 2011 statistics on Coke:

- 75% of revenues were from outside the U.S.

- 75% of profits were from outside the U.S.

- 53% of new capital investment was outside the U.S.

Coca Cola is a premier global growth company that would have peaked long ago if it was only a premier American growth company.

American multinational companies, like Coca Cola and hundreds of others, are the most thoroughly globalized companies in the world. They produce about twice as much outside their borders as European and Japanese multinationals.

Such geographic diversification helps U.S. companies smooth out the ups and downs internally. This is particularly true of investing in emerging markets. U.S.-based global companies are well positioned in these countries and take advantage of their strategic production advantages and their rising consumer spending.   U.S. companies' investment abroad has had a significant impact on both top lines (revenues) and their bottom lines (profits).

Investing in the U.S. large company asset class is investing globally with all of the major advantages of domestic investing intact.

International Investing Comes of Age

From the end of WWII through the end of the 20th century, the United States was the single dominant economic power. However, a dramatic change began with the new century.

The seeds of this change were planted with the opening up of China to outside trade in the 1980s and accelerated after the fall of the Berlin Wall in 1989, which the late Sir John Templeton called the third most important event in all of history. As a result of these changes, fully three billion people were added to our global capitalist system. The results were at first somewhat obscured by the technology revolution of the mid – late 1990s.

The changing economic landscape was certainly reflected in the bull market that went from late 2002 until late 2007. Even as U.S. stocks performed well, their returns were sub par compared to

European equities and positively dwarfed by returns from emerging markets.

Nothing epitomizes this change more than Warren Buffett. As stated earlier, he made only one foreign investment in his first forty-five years as an investment manager yet compiled perhaps the best investment track record ever over that period. Since 2002, Buffett has made a series of investments abroad and has been a cheerleader for foreign investing.

Most American investors have also awakened to the wider possibilities of diversifying into foreign stocks. However, as with any asset class, it is important to keep in mind that foreign equities will *underperform* U.S. stocks from time to time as cycles unfold. The calendar year of 2011 was a prime example. U.S. stock markets were slightly positive that year while international stock averages posted double digit declines.

The bottom line is that it has not been necessary to invest in foreign equities in order to achieve outstanding performance, yet, in a changing world, it is likely that investing in international stocks will become increasingly important for long-term investors. Introducing international stock ETFs and mutual funds into your Wealth and Retirement Portfolio may lower volatility and produce somewhat higher risk-adjusted rewards over time. This will be further evaluated in Section III.

International Cash and Bonds

The role of currencies is much more important for the holders of a foreign country's money market or bond investments. Any depreciation of a foreign country's currency will directly reduce the value of its bonds or cash equivalents in the hands of a U.S. investor without the potential for an offsetting benefit as illustrated in the discussion of foreign stocks. The reverse is also true. The appreciation of a country's currency is a direct benefit to the foreign holders of that country's bonds and cash.

Therefore, the long unwinding of the value of the U.S. dollar after 1971 was a huge and direct - if irregular - benefit to American holders of the major developed country's cash and bonds.

However, from 1995 to 2002, the U.S. dollar switched course and greatly appreciated in value relative to other major currencies. In this period, U.S. holders of international cash and bonds did not fare well.

By 2003, the U.S. Dollar was once again overvalued on a purchasing power parity basis relative to other major currencies. For the balance of the first decade of the new millennium, the Dollar generally depreciated. A notable exception was the period directly around the financial crisis at the end of 2008 and early 2009. At that time – as around other crisis situations – a "flight to quality" from around the world benefitted the U.S. Dollar.

Emerging market currencies have benefitted from their countries growing foreign reserves, relatively low government debt ratios, low entitlement commitments and younger populations.

Conclusion

Historically, U.S. stock investors could achieve most or all of their exposure to international growth through investing in leading U.S. multinational companies. Yet there are increasing opportunities available to direct international investing – particularly with the rise of emerging markets. Thus, international stocks – including emerging markets – should be an important piece of your Wealth and Retirement Portfolio.

Investing in international cash and bond markets is somewhat of a different story. In essence, these are as much currency speculation as they are a bond alternative. Such investments are best viewed tactically instead of as a long-term position in your Wealth and Retirement Portfolio.

5

Tangible Investments: REITs, Gold and Commodities

Introduction

Real estate investment trusts (REITs) offer a combination of risk and reward that can be a valuable addition to your Wealth and Retirement Portfolio.

The performance of gold tends to be extremely volatile while providing long periods of general outperformance versus other asset classes followed by equally long periods of underperformance. Commodities are a relatively new addition to the world of asset classes for *portfolio* investment. Unfortunately, it is also a difficult asset class to capture for most investors.

In the uncertain and cloudy investment environment since 2000, tangible asset classes – REITs and gold in particular – provided solid returns. Yet they did little to dampen downside volatility during the financial crisis.

"All that glitters is not gold."

— William Shakespeare,
The Merchant of Venice

Common stocks, bonds and cash equivalents are by far the most widely held financial investments by Americans, either directly or through mutual funds.

There is, however, one other group of asset classes that are often included in portfolios. These are the tangible asset classes. The three most widely available for Wealth and Retirement Portfolios are:

- REITs (Real Estate Investment Trusts)

- Gold and other Precious metals

- Commodities

REITs

Real estate investment trusts (REITs, pronounced "reets") are securitized real estate - listed securities that pool investors' money in all forms of real estate development, operations and/or lending. Typically the properties held by REITs are commercial real estate such as shopping centers and office buildings.

A REIT is like a mutual fund of real estate properties, typically offering investors a diversified portfolio with professional management. REITs are a special form of common stock and trade on stock exchanges. They offer "liquidity" and diversification to an otherwise illiquid real estate market.

Created by legislation passed in 1960, a REIT is essentially a corporation with special tax treatment. As investment companies, they can avoid income tax at the entity level by distributing out 90% of their taxable income to their shareholders. Most REITs generate substantial depreciation, so their cash flow is much higher than the taxable income they distribute. This allows many REITs to grow their asset base via new construction or new purchases over time. Still, it has been the relatively high yields from the distribution of their taxable income that is an essential and attractive feature of this asset class.

REITs have a checkered history in somewhat the same fashion as high-yield bonds. In their early years, REITs were a desirable source of capital for new realty development. A burst of enthusiasm in the late 1960s and early 1970s sent the microscopic base of REIT stocks soaring. Later in the 1970s, the real estate market went through a devastating crash that went from one geographical area to another and one property type to the next. As real estate was typically highly leveraged - and REIT developments in the 1970s were no exception - the entire REIT industry was devastated and their stock prices plummeted.

The REITs hit hardest were those referred to as *mortgage* REITs, which primarily lend money for commercial real estate development.

Chastened by this experience, most equity REITs have brought down their leverage ratios and most investors have focused on REITs which *own* the properties in their portfolios. Property types include Apartments, Offices, Industrial, Storage and Shopping Centers/Malls.

The National Association of Real Estate Investment Trusts (NAREIT) publishes several REIT indexes. From 1972 through 2011, the NAREIT equity index has outperformed the S&P 500 index. Importantly, this performance was also delivered with approximately the same volatility as that of the total U.S. stock market. However, the NAREIT index for all REITs (including mortgage and specialized REITs) has delivered substantially poorer performance. Therefore, only equity REITs shall be evaluated for possible inclusion in your Wealth and Retirement Portfolio.

Note: The equity REIT performance is subject to qualification. In the REIT indexes published by NAREIT, "Only those REITs listed for the entire period are used in the Total Return calculation." In other words, delisted, bankrupt or merged REITs disappear from the index *without* accounting for their performance in the last month of their existence. How much impact this has had on performance is impossible to calculate.

The Rapid Growth of Equity REITs

The amount of publicly traded real estate has grown rapidly. The equity REIT asset class is still relatively small, totaling only about $438 billion at the end of 2011 (compared to the total stock market capitalization of $15.6 trillion), yet it has grown substantially from a mere $9 billion base at the end of 1991. As the market has grown, so has the liquidity. About $5 billion in REITs trade each day, about 100 times as much as in 1992.

For years, large pension plans have allocated a portion of their investment portfolios to real estate. Increasingly, these pension plans are turning to REITs to fill out this allocation. This not only fuels demand for REITs but also helps stabilize the market as large pension plans tend to be patient, long-term holders of their investment assets.

The Maturing Public Real Estate Industry

From inception until the early 1990s, most equity REITs were little more than securitized ownership of specific properties. After a severe downturn in 1989 and 1990, the REIT has reinvented itself. Today, most are bigger, stronger and deeper than earlier models. The new model is that of a fully integrated real estate company. These companies have developed talented organizations that can acquire, manage, lease and develop commercial real estate.

The new model has opportunities to add value and increase cash flow from each activity within the organization. As the industry grows, it is also consolidating around ever bigger entities. Larger REITs are taking advantage of economies of scale and a lower cost of capital. This has not gone without notice. REITs were included in the S&P 500 Index in 2002.

The future of REITs looks quite promising. The commercial real estate market in America alone is huge, being not too much smaller than the stock market by total market valuation. Yet it is still largely in private hands. Over time, a large portion of commercial real estate may find its way into public REITs. This is good for investors, too.

Publicly traded real estate securities offer ordinary investors access to real estate investment on terms that are typically more economical and favorable than direct property investment partnerships.

Gold and other Precious Metals

Gold and other precious metals are either speculations or monetary assets (currency alternatives), not traditional investments. Investments are income-producing. Speculations and currencies produce no income and therefore must rely on real or perceived changes in the relationship between supply and demand to effect a change in price. In other words, there is no discounting of future dividends or earnings to arrive at a fair estimation of present value as there is with stocks, REITs or bonds.

Gold and silver tend to make sharp moves up and down in the short run, yet often just match prevailing inflation over long periods of time.

From 1972 through 2011, gold produced an average annualized return of approximately 9.9%, about equal to the U.S. stock market. The reality is that this return for gold was artificially produced. From the end of 1935 to 1971, the inflation rate averaged 3.2% per year. Yet gold's price could not adjust to inflation as it was held constant at $35 per ounce by government decree. Had gold's price been allowed free-market pricing, it is likely that its price would have been closer to $115 per ounce in 1971. From that price in 1971, gold would have returned 6.5% annually (instead of 9.9%) through the end of 2011. Compared to the 4.4% annual inflation over that period, this was a *real* return of just a little over 2% annually.

This performance by gold might appear to be inconsistent with gold's history as merely an inflation hedge - or store of stable value. Whereas this is certainly true when measured by "purchasing power" over the centuries, it does not mean that gold has not underperformed and outperformed inflation for many decades in a row over time.

Two factors have heavily influenced gold's price movement over shorter periods of time:

- Supply and Demand shocks

- Government intervention

Both gold and silver prices have been negatively impacted by supply shocks from time to time over history. Typically, this has come from a major new supply source becoming available. Some historical examples include the Spanish "finding" gold in South America in the 1500s, the gold rush in America in the mid-1800s and the South African gold rush in the late 1800s. Dramatic new supplies of gold tend to deflate the value of gold – or conversely, inflate the value of everything else that is priced in gold.

Periodic demand shocks have positively impacted the price of gold and silver and other precious metals. Such shocks are often caused by major political disruption such as the Russian revolution in the 1920s that caused mass purchases of easily transported gold by the wealthy as they fled Russia. We have recently seen similar actions connected to the so called Arab Spring which has affected many countries in the Mideast.

Another recent demand shock has developed in China. China's rapid growth over the past several decades has created a wealthy class in China. In addition, the recent dramatic wage increases of industrial workers there have created a whole new middle class. Both the rich and middle class in China are great savers. However, because of their immature financial system, they have little access to the plethora of financial products we take for granted in developed countries. In addition, interests paid on deposits are very low (by government decree) and real estate is richly valued. All together, these have helped gold to be an investment of choice in China. So much so that in 2011

China passed India as the number one source of gold demand worldwide.

The other major influence on the price of gold is government intervention – both direct and indirect. Direct actions include setting the official price of gold in the country's currency; confiscating gold (making it illegal for private citizens to own it); and buying or selling gold in the open market. Indirect actions by governments include "printing money" (creating currency and reserves faster than needed by the economy) thus creating inflationary pressure.

It is the unique response of gold's price to demand shocks and government actions that makes it a valuable addition to your Wealth and Retirement Portfolio.

Adding to today's economic uncertainty is that virtually all major nations – both developed and emerging – want to keep their currencies "weak" against other country's currencies. This boosts their export competitiveness and helps reduce the true cost of the large debt loads that most countries have built up since the financial crisis of 2008-2009. Of course, not every country can have a weak currency versus all others at the same time, however they can all weaken their currencies versus gold – a non-government sponsored monetary "currency". And this is exactly what has happened. This also makes gold a unique diversifier versus the "paper" currencies issued by governments.

Finally, we live in a world where a major terrorist event could unsettle the markets for stocks, bonds and real estate but which would likely positively impact the price of gold. Thus it has an important role as a diversifying asset class in this uncertain environment.

Commodities

As an asset class, commodities cover a wide variety of subgroups including grains, livestock, industrial metals, and energy fuels.

Many of these commodities have been on some form of exchange for centuries. In essence, these exchanges were set up to allow farmers, ranchers and miners the opportunity to "sell forward" or "hedge" their product's price long before it was delivered for sale.

Commodities were not commonly considered an asset class for inclusion in either an individual or institutional portfolio until the early 2000s. By that time, financial products had been developed that allowed investors to basically mimic the price of the underlying commodities in a *relatively* efficient manner. Obviously, most investors do not want to own or be liable to take delivery of the underlying products themselves.

But what really spurred investors' demand for commodities was the dissemination of research studies suggesting that major commodity indexes had long term returns similar to stocks but with little correlation or similarity to the timing of stock's ups and downs.[1] In other words, a portfolio of stocks and commodities would have similar long term returns to either asset class alone, but with less volatility. (Correlation will be discussed in more detail in Section III.)

A second attraction of commodities is as an inflation hedge. This was certainly the case in the 1970s when virtually each commodity subgroup performed especially well in that decade's high inflation.

As appealing as the perceived lack of correlation and inflation hedge characteristics are, there are many features of the commodities asset class that make it less than ideal for your Wealth and Retirement Portfolio. These include:

- Commodities are a speculation, not an investment, as was discussed with gold. They do not have earnings, dividends or interest.

---

[1] Weiser, Stefan (2003, "The Strategic Case for Commodities in Portfolio Diversification." *Commodities Now.*
Erb, Claude B and Campbell R. Harvey (2005), "The Tactical and Strategic Value of Commodity Futures," Duke University.

- Increased volatility – Most major commodity indexes demonstrated significantly higher volatility than either stocks or bonds in the first decade of the 2000s. (Morgan Stanley, Investment Focus, 2/2010).

- Contango effect – Most of the stellar returns from commodity indexes occurred when "backwardization" was the norm, i.e. the price of the commodity in the future, based on its futures contract, was cheaper than the current or spot price. This created a very positive roll feature for the return from commodity *futures contracts* (The basic investment vehicle for both individual and institutional portfolio investments). This means that a commodity's futures contract would generally rise in value, as it approached maturity. However, in recent years, many commodities have been in "contango" – or negative roll – with futures prices higher than spot prices and thus creating a headwind for returns.

- Wrong correlations – Commodities have not been a good portfolio diversifier when one needs it most – during economic downturns. This was particularly true during the heart of the financial crisis in 2008.

- Short history – Most commodity indexes have only been available in real time since the mid – 1990s. Prior performance of these indexes were from backtesting available data which is not nearly as accurate.

Given these important limitations and qualifiers,, commodities are not deemed to be an essential asset class for inclusion in your Wealth and Retirement Portfolio. However, tactical investors may find commodity vehicles they feel comfortable with and appropriate market conditions to warrant using them.

Conclusion

Tangible investments can play an important role in a well-diversified portfolio. Gold has very special characteristics as a monetary alternative to paper currencies as well as its inflation hedging capability.

REITs have developed one of the best risk/reward profiles of any asset class and deserve to be included in your Wealth and Retirement Portfolio.

Commodities, as pointed out just above, have too many caveats and limitations to warrant permanent inclusion in your Wealth and Retirement Portfolio.

6

Measuring Risks and Rewards

Introduction

Chapters 2 through 5 of this section provided a discussion of the major asset classes - both their advantages and limitations. This chapter will introduce a methodology for more precisely measuring the long-term risks and rewards that each major asset class has offered. It will answer the question, *"How much reward has each asset class delivered for the risks incurred?"*

In the uncertain world of investing, it is critical to have a methodology that has worked – even in and after the financial crisis of 2008 – 2009. Predictable risk/reward relationships are comforting to those seeking as much certainty as possible from their long-term investment portfolio.

> *"Nothing has really changed on Wall Street over the years. In fact, much of what happens in the financial world today has been played over in history many times before and has been captured in the cycles and trends of financial charts created over time."*
>
> - Ken Fisher, *The Wall Street Waltz*, 1987

The Enigma of Risk

The long history of major asset classes reveals an important fact: *not one has ever sustained a permanent loss.* Eventually, every decline in value has been recovered. However, any decline in market value can be turned into a permanent loss. For example, many investors sold their equity mutual funds right after the 1987 crash, others toward the end of the 2008-2009 financial crises. These investors were not properly prepared for the magnitude of those declines - even though they fell well within historic parameters.

The purpose of understanding the risks within each asset class is to be both intellectually and emotionally prepared for the range and intensity of its inevitable market declines. A special part of this preparation is to come to grips with the entirely random nature of these market declines. *Neither the timing nor the intensity (within a range) of the next decline can be predicted.*

Therefore, the better an investor is prepared for the entire range of expected declines in a particular asset class (based upon its longest period of documented history), the more likely his actions will serve his own best long-term interests. Either he will not invest in a particular asset class in the first place or he will stay the course during its inevitable declines.

The study of the risks within any particular asset class thus becomes the study of the severity, frequency and duration of its declines in market value.

The academic measurement of risk is called standard deviation,[1] which is not an investor-friendly tool. It falls short of providing a real appreciation for the risk in owning a particular investment. In fact, standard deviation is not a measurement of market declines per se, it is a measurement of the annual volatility or degree of variance an investment experiences in producing a particular

---

[1] A complete discussion of standard deviation is given in the Appendix, page 248.

average rate of return. Upside movements are as influential as downside movements in its calculation.

Therefore, right from the beginning, standard deviation *fails* as a measurement of market *declines*. Standard deviation does provide an insight into the normalized distribution of *annual* returns, but it fails to prepare investors for the full range of the declines they will likely incur over a lifetime of investing. A more useful measurement of risk is required to fulfill the mission of preparing investors for the declines in market value they face over long investment periods.

Long-Term Risk: Bear Markets

Risk, the intensity of market declines within an asset class, can be measured over a variety of time periods. As this book takes a long-term perspective, it will focus on those major market declines that occur infrequently (about once every five years on average). These substantial setbacks in market value, often referred to as bear markets, tend to be the major concern of most *investors* as opposed to the short-term ups and downs that preoccupy *traders*.

Actually, the history of asset classes shows that there are two types of bear markets. First, there are the normal cyclical bear markets that tend to be sharp and short-term. Then there are the very infrequent major bear markets that tend to be much deeper and more prolonged. The major bear markets induce more than concern from investors, they instill real fear. The S&P 500 has endured five such major bear market declines since 1925, the Depression Era crash of 1929 - 1932, the Depression Relapse of 1937-1941, the Inflation Era's monetary crisis of 1973-1974, the aftermath of the 1990s bubble from 2000-2002, and the major bear market of 2007-2009 that accompanied the financial crisis.

For the S&P 500 Index, the average of the last three major bear markets was a 46% decline (based on month-end data). The remaining bear market declines since 1960 averaged a 20% decline. A more detailed discussion of the Risk Profile and bear markets begins on page 87. These bear market characteristics are of great value when comparing different asset classes.

Long-Term Rewards

Financial performance is a combination of risk and reward. Whereas risk is multifaceted, the reward from investing is fairly easy to identify. The reward of owning any asset class or portfolio is the rate of return it has delivered *above* that of the riskless 30-day U.S. Treasury bill.

Reward = Rate of Return on Asset Class *less* the
Rate of Return on Cash (T-bills)

Every investor can purchase a 30-day U.S. Treasury bill (the cash asset class) and receive the riskless return it offers. The return from cash therefore sets the base from which reward is measured. Your reward from an investment is only that *extra* return (above the riskless return of cash) for which you must incur some amount of bear market risk. *In other words, your return is only meaningful in relationship to the risk taken to achieve it!*

For example, the Reward from owning the S&P 500 for the 1972-2011 period was 4.4%. This is simply the 9.8% average annual total return of the S&P 500 for this period *less* the 5.4% average annual return offered by Treasury bills in that same period.

Historical Risk/Reward Charts

As stated earlier, "the purpose of understanding the risks within each asset class is to be both intellectually and emotionally prepared for the range and intensity of its inevitable market declines." The best preparation is to see and feel the major declines in market value that each asset class has experienced over its history and then to envision living through those setbacks as if they were occurring in your own investment in the years ahead.

The Historical Risk/Reward chart allows you to do just that. On a single page, it walks you through the month-by-month history of the asset class, segregating the bear markets and the bull markets. Spending just a few minutes studying a Historical Risk/Reward chart will greatly add to your appreciation of the relationship between the risks and reward within that asset class.

Historical Risk/Reward Chart for the S&P 500

Chart 6-1 is a Historical Risk/Reward chart of the S&P 500 for the period beginning in 1972. One hundred thousand dollars ($100,000) invested in the S&P 500 on January 1, 1972, grew to $4,249,000 by December 31, 2011. The equivalent value of an investment in cash (30-day T-bills) was $825,900.   The S&P 500 produced an accumulated return that was over five times that from cash. (Both assume that all interest, dividends and capital gains were reinvested and that taxes were not taken out.)

The computation of the Reward of owning the S&P 500 is shown on the bottom left side of this chart, while its Risk Profile is shown on the bottom right side.

To achieve these superior results, an investor in the S&P 500 lived through periods of significant setbacks which are highlighted as the solid red areas on the chart. These are the bear markets that long-term owners must take in stride.

As you can see, the magnitude of these bear market declines varies widely from a mild 15% setback to an ugly 51% decline. Also notice that bear markets in the S&P 500 were as short as two months and as long as 25 months. The lightly shaded sections following each bear market show how long it took to recover the temporary loss of that decline. These periods vary sharply too. The entire solid area plus the following lightly shaded area together indicate the total length of time an investor was *underwater* from a prior high in market value. The white areas denote major periods of net new advancement.

The combined lightly shaded areas (recovery periods) and the white areas (net new advancement) together represent the bull markets that follow the bear markets (solid areas). One bull market plus one bear market (in either order) is a *full market cycle.*

Standard and Poor's 500
Growth of $100,000
(12/31/71 – 12/31/11)

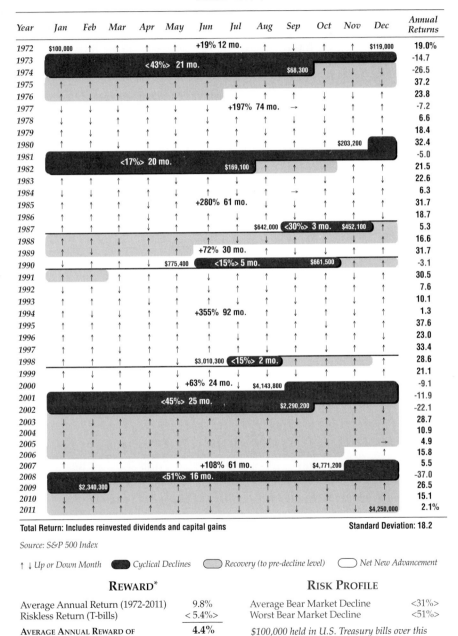

Year	Jan	Feb	Mar	Apr	May	Jun	Jul	Aug	Sep	Oct	Nov	Dec	Annual Returns
1972	$100,000	↑	↑	↑	↑	+19% 12 mo.		↑	↓	↑	↑	$119,000	19.0%
1973				<43%> 21 mo.									-14.7
1974									$68,300	↑	↓	↓	-26.5
1975	↑	↑	↑	↑	↑	↑	↓	↓	↓	↓	↑	↑	37.2
1976	↑	↓	↓	↓	↓	↑	↓	↑	↑	↓	↓	↑	23.8
1977	↓	↓	↓	↑	↓	↓	+197% 74 mo.	→	↓	↑	↑	↑	-7.2
1978	↓	↓	↑	↑	↑	↓	↑	↑	↓	↓	↑	↑	6.6
1979	↑	↓	↑	↑	↓	↑	↑	↑	↓	↑	↓	↑	18.4
1980	↑	↑	↓	↑	↑	↑	↑	↑	↑	↑	$203,200	↑	32.4
1981													-5.0
1982			<17%> 20 mo.			$169,100	↑	↑	↑	↑	↑	↑	21.5
1983	↑	↑	↑	↑	↓	↑	↓	↑	↑	↓	↑	↓	22.6
1984	↓	↓	↑	↑	↓	↑	↓	↑	→	↑	↓	↑	6.3
1985	↑	↑	↑	↓	↑	+280% 61 mo.	↓	↓	↓	↑	↑	↑	31.7
1986	↑	↑	↑	↓	↑	↑	↓	↑	↓	↑	↑	↓	18.7
1987	↑	↑	↑	↓	↑	↑	↑	$642,000	<30%> 3 mo.	$452,100	↑	↑	5.3
1988	↑	↑	↓	↑	↓	↑	↓	↓	↑	↑	↓	↑	16.6
1989	↑	↓	↑	↑	↑	+72% 30 mo.	↑	↑	↓	↓	↑	↑	31.7
1990	↓	↑	↑	↓	$775,400	<15%> 5 mo.	↑	↓	↓	$661,500	↑	↑	-3.1
1991	↑	↑	↑	↑	↑	↓	↑	↑	↓	↓	↓	↑	30.5
1992	↓	↑	↓	↑	↑	↓	↑	↓	↑	↑	↑	↑	7.6
1993	↑	↑	↑	↓	↑	↑	↓	↑	↓	↑	↓	↑	10.1
1994	↑	↓	↓	↑	↑	+355% 92 mo.	↑	↑	↓	↑	↓	↑	1.3
1995	↑	↑	↑	↑	↑	↑	↑	↓	↑	↓	↑	↑	37.6
1996	↑	↑	↑	↑	↑	↑	↓	↑	↑	↑	↑	↓	23.0
1997	↑	↑	↓	↑	↑	↑	↑	↓	↑	↓	↑	↑	33.4
1998	↑	↑	↑	↑	↓	$3,010,300	<15%> 2 mo.	↑	↑	↑	↑	↑	28.6
1999	↑	↓	↑	↑	↓	↑	↓	↓	↓	↑	↑	↑	21.1
2000	↓	↓	↑	↓	↑	+63% 24 mo.	↓	↑	↓	$4,143,800	↓	↓	-9.1
2001				<45%> 25 mo.					↓	$2,290,200	↑	↑	-11.9
2002	↓	↓	↑	↓	↓	↓	↓	↑	↓	↑	↑	↓	-22.1
2003	↓	↓	↑	↑	↑	↑	↑	↑	↓	↑	↑	↑	28.7
2004	↑	↑	↓	↓	↑	↑	↓	↑	↑	↑	↑	↑	10.9
2005	↓	↑	↓	↓	↑	↑	↑	↓	↑	↓	↑	→	4.9
2006	↑	↑	↑	↑	↓	↑	↑	↑	↑	↑	↑	↑	15.8
2007	↑	↓	↑	↑	↑	+108% 61 mo.	↑	↑	$4,771,200	↑	↓	↓	5.5
2008				<51%> 16 mo.									-37.0
2009	$2,340,300	↑	↑	↑	↑	↓	↑	↑	↑	↑	↑	↑	26.5
2010	↓	↑	↑	↑	↓	↓	↑	↓	↑	↑	↑	↑	15.1
2011	↑	↑	↑	↑	↓	↓	↓	↓	↓	↑	↓	$4,250,000	2.1%

Total Return: Includes reinvested dividends and capital gains   **Standard Deviation: 18.2**

Source: S&P 500 Index

↑ ↓ Up or Down Month   ⬛ Cyclical Declines   ⬭ Recovery (to pre-decline level)   ⬭ Net New Advancement

REWARD*		RISK PROFILE	
Average Annual Return (1972-2011)	9.8%	Average Bear Market Decline	<31%>
Riskless Return (T-bills)	<5.4%>	Worst Bear Market Decline	<51%>
AVERAGE ANNUAL REWARD OF STANDARD AND POOR'S 500	**4.4%**	*$100,000 held in U.S. Treasury bills over this time period grew to $825,900.*	

Annualized. ©2012 by Tanglewood Capital Management, Inc.

CHART 6-1

The percentage gain and the number of months over which the bull markets unfolded are reflected in the numbers on the chart. These also varied widely in degree and duration. The smallest full bull market was up 63% over a period of less than three years. The largest is the 355% bull market of 1991-1998 which is also the longest of this period.

The up and down arrows show whether that particular month-end value was up or down from the prior month. Directly below the chart, the standard deviation for the S&P 500 (18.2 for the period of 1972-2011) is also shown.

The current value of an initial $100,000 portfolio (beginning January 1, 1972) is shown at the end of each bull market and at the bottom of each bear market. This provides you an excellent view of where your month-end brokerage statements were heading in each major advance and each major decline. Visualize your own S&P 500 investment going through similar advances - and particularly declines - in the future. The intent is to prepare you today for what is likely to unfold in some random sequence in the decades ahead.

As you can see, the history of the S&P 500 is one of continuous progress punctuated by periodic setbacks of varying intensity.

A Powerful Predictor

Long-term investors who have armed themselves with Historical Risk/Reward charts have a powerful advantage - they know what types of risks and rewards have occurred in the past and are most likely to incur in the years ahead. They understand the major risks of ownership.

A Historical Risk/Reward chart is like a peek into the future of that asset class. All of the declines shown on its chart will likely unfold again - only in some unforeseen and random sequence. The good news is that the reward, too, is likely to repeat over the long haul.

Conclusion

The Historical Risk Reward chart introduced in this chapter is designed to give you a thorough understanding of both the risks and rewards of the asset class being studied.

In chapter 7 we will put this evaluation tool to good use as we evaluate all of the major asset classes that are well suited for permanent inclusion in your Wealth and Retirement Portfolio and compare their risk/reward characteristics.

7

Comparing Risks and Rewards of Major Asset Classes

Introduction

Chapter six introduced a methodology for examining an asset class in terms of its historic risks and rewards. In this chapter, we will use this methodology to compare the individual risks and rewards of the major asset classes that survived our evaluations in Chapters two through five.

Now the various asset classes can be compared on an apples-to-apples basis. In an uncertain world, we are seeking as much certainty as possible.

> *"At heart, America is a nation of careful gamblers. The contradictions in that description are rooted in our national character as a people who know instinctively that no gain is achieved without both risks and costs....The secret of our success, indeed the key to democracy itself, is in striking the balance between risk and rewards...."*
>
> — Senator Nancy Kassebaum

All of the asset classes compared in this chapter have index-quality data back to January 1, 1972, (Chart 7-1). This is basically the longest period for which all of these asset classes can be fairly compared during the same market conditions. This 40-year period of market history was rich in variation - major bull and bear markets, rising and falling inflation, high and low interest rates and stagnant and growing periods for the world economy. This is, therefore, an excellent period to use as the basis of comparison.

Asset Class	*Index Source*
U.S. Stocks	**CRSP** (1972-1980); **Russell** (1981-2011)
Total U.S. Bond Market	Barcap **U.S. Aggregate Bond Index** (1976-2011); **Long-Term U.S. Corporate Bond Index** (1972-1975)
Intermediate Treasury Bonds	CRSP(1972-1980); **Citigroup** (1981-2011)
Cash (30-day U.S. T-bills)	Ibbotson/ Thomson Financial (1972 – 2011)
International Stocks	**FTSE All World less U.S.** (1994-2011) **Morgan Stanley/MSCI** (1972-1993);
Equity REITs	**NAREIT** (1972 – 2011)
Gold	**London: Gold (Thomson)** (1972 – 2011)

CHART 7-1

Index Descriptions:

U.S. Stocks: The Russell 3000 index measures the total return of the 3,000 largest companies in the US. This index is reconstituted annually. The index is adjusted for free float and liquidity so the benchmark reflects the shares that are actually available on the open market.

REITS: The National Association of Real Estate Investment Trusts (NAREIT), Equity REIT index, which measures the total return of most REITS which own, or have an "equity interest" in rental real estate.

International Stocks: The FTSE All World ex US Index is designed to help US investors benchmark their international investments. This ETF comprises Large and Mid-cap stocks providing coverage of both Developed and Emerging Markets (46 countries) *excluding* the US. The underlying index is adjusted for free float and liquidity so the benchmark reflects the shares that are actually available on the open market.

Bonds:
A) The Barclay's US Aggregate Index covers the US Dollar denominated, investment grade, fixed rate, and taxable areas of the bond market. This is the broadest measure of the taxable US bond market, including most Treasury, agency, corporate, mortgage-backed, asset-backed, and international dollar-denominated issues, all with investment grade ratings and maturities of 1 year or more.
B) The Barclays Capital 5-Year U.S. Treasury Bellwethers Index is an unmanaged universe of 5 Yr Treasury bonds, and used as a benchmark against the market for intermediate-term maturity fixed-income securities. The index assumes reinvestment of all distributions and interest payments.

Gold: The London Fix Gold PM Price, the internationally recognized benchmark for gold prices set by the members of the London Bullion Market Association. It is based on actual buy and sell orders for gold in the global market.

Cash: The Citigroup 1 Month Treasury Bill Index is a market value weighted index of public obligations of the US Treasury with maturities of 1 month.

Historical Risk/Rewards

A Historical Risk/Reward chart is presented for each of the asset classes in the following pages 7-2 through 7-7.

The risks and rewards of these asset classes are summarized in Chart 7-8 and Chart 7-9.

Total Domestic Stock Market
Growth of $100,000
(12/31/71 – 12/31/11)

Year	Jan	Feb	Mar	Apr	May	Jun	Jul	Aug	Sep	Oct	Nov	Dec	Annual Returns
1972	$100,000	↑	↑	↑	↑	+17% 12 mo.		↑	↓	↑	↑	$116,900	16.9%
1973					<45%> 21 mo.								-18.1
1974									$64,000	↑	↓	↓	-27.2
1975	↑	↑	↑	↑	↑	↑	↓	↓	↑	↑	↑	↓	38.7
1976	↑	↑	↑	↓	↑	↑	↓	↑	↑	↓	↑	↑	26.7
1977	↓	↓	↓	↑	↓	+228% 78 mo.		↓	↑	↓	↑	↑	-4.2
1978	↓	↓	↑	↑	↑	↓	↑	↑	↓	↓	↑	↑	7.5
1979	↑	↓	↑	↑	↓	↑	↑	↑	↑	↓	↑	↑	23.0
1980	↑	↑	↓	↑	↑	↑	↑	+44% 12 mo.		↑	↑	↓	32.7
1981	↓	↑	$209,700										-4.4
1982				<17%> 16 mo.			$174,700			↑	↑	↑	20.7
1983	↑	↑	↑	↑	↑	↓	↓	↑	↑	↓	↑	↓	22.7
1984	↓	↓	↑	↑	↓	↑	↓	↑	↑	↑	↓	↑	3.4
1985	↑	↑	↓	↓	↑	+260% 61 mo.		↓	↓	↑	↑	↑	32.2
1986	↑	↑	↑	↓	↑	↑	↓	↑	↓	↑	↑	↓	16.7
1987	↑	↑	↑	↓	↑	↑	↑	$629,300	<30%> 3 mo.	$441,500	↓	↑	1.9
1988	↑	↑	↓	↑	↓	↑	↓	↓	↑	↑	↓	↑	17.8
1989	↑	↓	↑	↑	↑	+68% 30 mo.		↑	↓	↓	↑	↑	29.3
1990	↓	↑	↑	↓	$743,300	<16%> 5 mo.			$622,600	↑	↑	↑	-5.0
1991	↑	↑	↑	↑	↑	↓	↑	↑	↓	↓	↓	↑	33.7
1992	↓	↑	↓	↑	↑	↓	↑	↓	↑	↑	↑	↑	9.7
1993	↑	↑	↑	↓	↑	+354% 92 mo.		↑	↑	↑	↓	↑	10.9
1994	↑	↓	↓	↑	↑	↓	↑	↑	↓	↑	↓	↑	0.2
1995	↑	↑	↑	↑	↑	↑	↑	↑	↑	↓	↑	↑	36.8
1996	↑	↑	↑	↑	↑	↑	↓	↑	↑	↑	↑	↓	21.8
1997	↑	↑	↓	↑	↑	↑	↑	↓	↑	↓	↑	↑	31.8
1998	↑	↑	↑	↑	↓	$2,823,800	<17%> 2 mo.		↑	↑	↑	↑	24.1
1999	↑	↓	↑	↑	↓	+67% 24 mo.		↓	↓	↑	↑	↑	20.9
2000	↓	↑	↑	↓	↓	↑	↓	$3,921,800					-7.5
2001				<44%> 25 mo.									-11.5
2002							$2,190,900			↑	↑	↑	-21.5
2003	↓	↓	↑	↑	↑	↑	↑	↑	↑	↑	↑	↑	31.0
2004	↑	↑	↓	↓	↑	↑	↓	↑	↑	↑	↑	↑	11.9
2005	↓	↑	↓	↓	↑	↑	↑	↓	↑	↓	↑	↓	6.1
2006	↑	↑	↑	↑	↓	+115% 61 mo.		↑	↑	↑	↑	↑	15.7
2007	↑	↓	↑	↑	↑	↓	↓	↑	↑	$4,716,700			5.1
2008				<51%> 16 mo.					°				-37.3
2009	$2,302,000	↑	↑	↑	↑	↑	↑	↑	↑	↓	↑	↑	28.3
2010	↑	↑	↑	↑	↓	↓	↑	↓	↓	↑	↑	↑	16.9
2011	↑	↑	↑	↑	↓	↓	↓	↓	↓	↑	↓	$4,255,200	1.0%

Total Return: Includes reinvested dividends and capital gains   Standard Deviation: 18.4

Source: Center for Research in Security Pricing (CRSP) University of Chicago through 1980; Russell 3000 Index 1981-2011

↑↓ Up or Down Month   ● Cyclical Declines   ● Recovery (to pre-decline level)   ○ Net New Advancement

REWARD*

Average Annual Return (1972-2011)	9.8%
Riskless Return (T-bills)	< 5.4%>
AVERAGE ANNUAL REWARD OF TOTAL DOMESTIC MARKET	**4.4%**

RISK PROFILE

Average Bear Market Decline	<31%>
Worst Bear Market Decline	<51%>

$100,000 held in U.S. Treasury bills over this time period grew to $825,900.

Annualized. ©2012 by Tanglewood Capital Management, Inc.

CHART 7-2

Government Bonds (5-Year Treasury)
Growth of $100,000
(12/31/71 – 12/31/11)

Year	Jan	Feb	Mar	Apr	May	Jun	Jul	Aug	Sep	Oct	Nov	Dec	Annual Returns
1972	$100,000	↑	↑	↑	↑	↑	↑	↑	↑	↑	↑	↑	5.2%
1973	↓	↓	↑	↑	↑	+11% 26 mo.	↑	↑	↑	↑	↑	↑	4.6
1974	↑	$110,500	<4%> 2 mo.	↑	↓	↓	↑	↓	↑	↑	↑	↑	5.7
1975	↑	↑	↓	↓	↑	↑	↓	↓	↑	↑	↓	↑	7.8
1976	↑	↑	↑	↑	↓	↑	↑	↑	↑	↑	↑	↑	12.9
1977	↓	↓	↑	↓	↑	+47% 62 mo.	↑	↑	↑	↑	↑	↑	1.4
1978	↑	↑	↑	→	↓	↑	↑	↑	↓	↑	↑	3.5
1979	↑	↓	↑	↑	↑	$156,100	↑	<9%> 8 mo.	↑	↑	↑	•	4.1
1980	$142,700	+19% 3 mo.	$170,000	<9%> 15 mo.									3.9
1981	↑	↑	↑	↑	↑	$156,100	↑	↑	↑	↑	↑	↓	8.4
1982	↑	↑	↑	↑	↑	↓	↑	↑	↑	↑	↑	↑	28.2
1983	↑	↑	↓	↑	+53% 29 mo.	↑	↑	↑	↑	↑	↑	↑	5.4
1984	$239,300	<4%> 4 mo.	$230,200	↑	↑	↑	↑	↑	↑	↑	15.0
1985	↑	↑	↓	↑	↑	↑	↓	+63% 33 mo.	↑	↑	↑	↑	21.0
1986	↑	↓	↑	↑	↓	↑	↑	↑	↓	↑	↑	↓	13.0
1987	↑	$375,500	<5%> 7 mo.					$355,800	↑	↓	→	1.1
1988	↑	↑	↓	↓	↓	↑	↓	↓	↑	↑	↓	↓	5.4
1989	↑	↓	↑	↑	↑	↑	↑	↓	↑	↑	↑	↑	13.3
1990	↓	↑	↑	↓	↑	↑	↑	↓	↑	↑	↑	↑	8.9
1991	↑	↑	↑	↑	+85% 76 mo.	↑	↑	↑	↑	↑	↑	↑	14.6
1992	↓	↓	↓	↑	↑	↑	↑	↑	↑	↓	↑	↑	6.2
1993	↑	↑	↑	↑	↓	↑	↑	↑	↑	↑	↓	↑	9.7
1994	$658,000	<6%> 10 mo.								$620,400	↑	-4.0
1995	↑	↑	↑	↑	↑	↑	↓	↑	↑	↑	↑	↑	17.0
1996	↑	↓	↓	↓	↓	↑	+43% 50 mo.	↑	↑	↑	↑	↓	2.4
1997	↑	↑	↓	↑	↑	↑	↑	↓	↑	↑	↑	↑	7.9
1998	↑	↓	↑	↑	↑	↑	↑	↑	↑	↓	↓	↑	9.6
1999	$886,800	<3%> 6 mo.				$861,500	↑	↑	↑	↓	↑	↑	-2.6
2000	↓	↑	↑	↓	↑	↑	↑	↑	↑	↑	↑	↑	11.6
2001	↑	↑	↑	↓	↑	↑	↑	↑	↑	↑	↓	↓	7.7
2002	↑	↑	↓	↑	↑	↑	↑	↑	↑	↓	↓	↑	12.4
2003	↑	↑	↓	↑	↑	↓	→	↑	↑	↓	↓	↑	2.2
2004	↑	↑	↑	↓	+69% 104 mo.	↑	↑	↑	↑	↑	↓	↑	2.4
2005	↓	↓	↑	↑	↑	↑	↓	↑	↓	↓	↑	↑	0.0
2006	↓	↑	↓	↓	↑	↑	↑	↑	↑	↑	↑	↓	2.5
2007	↓	↑	↑	↑	↓	↑	↑	↑	↑	↑	↑	↑	10.2
2008	↑	↑	$1,452,400	<4%> 2 mo.	↑	↑	↑	↑	↑	↑	↑	↑	14.1
2009	↓	↓	↑	↓	↓	↓	↑	↑	↑	↓	↑	↓	-1.4
2010	↑	↑	↓	↑	↑	↑	↑	↑	↑	↑	↓	↓	6.9
2011	↑	↓	↓	↑	↑	↑	↑	↑	↑	↑	↑	$1,807,600	9.2%

Total Return: Includes reinvested interest   **Standard Deviation: 6.5**

Source: Center for Research in Security Pricing (CRSP) University of Chicago through 1980; Citigroup 5-year Treasury Benchmark 1981-2011

↑ ↓ Up or Down Month   ⬤ Cyclical Declines   ⬤ Recovery (to pre-decline level)   ◯ Net New Advancement

REWARD*

Average Annual Return (1972-2011)	7.5%
Riskless Return (T-bills)	<5.4%>
AVERAGE ANNUAL REWARD OF GOVERNMENT BONDS (5-YEAR TREASURY)	**2.1%**

RISK PROFILE

Average Bear Market Decline	<6%>
Worst Bear Market Decline	<9%>

$100,000 held in U.S. Treasury bills over this time period grew to $825,900.

*Annualized. ©2012 by Tanglewood Capital Management, Inc.

CHART 7-3

Total Bonds
Growth of $100,000
(12/31/71 – 12/31/11)

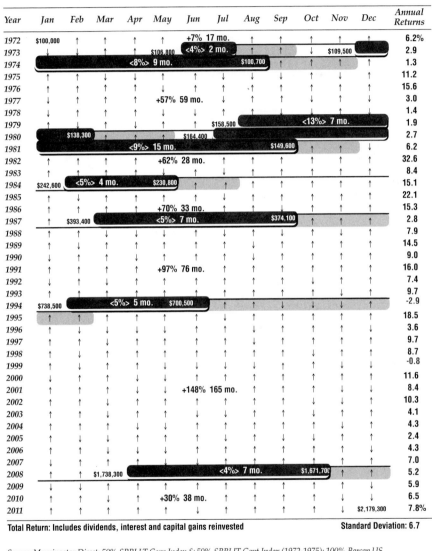

Year	Jan	Feb	Mar	Apr	May	Jun	Jul	Aug	Sep	Oct	Nov	Dec	Annual Returns
1972	$100,000	↑	↑	↑	↑	+7% 17 mo.		↑	↑	↑	↑		6.2%
1973	↑	↑	↑	$106,800	<4%> 2 mo.		↑	↑	↓	$109,500			2.9
1974	<8%> 9 mo.						$100,700	↑	↑	↑	↑		1.3
1975	↑	↑	↓	↓	↑	↑	↑	↓	↑	↑	↓	↑	11.2
1976	↑	↑	↑	↑	↓	↑	↑	·↑	↑	↑	↑	↑	15.6
1977	↓	↑	↑	↑	+57% 59 mo.		↓	↑	↑	↓	↑	↑	3.0
1978	↓	↑	↑	↑	↓	↓	↑	↑	↑	↑	↑	↑	1.4
1979	↑	↑	↑	↓	↑	↑	$158,500		↑	<13%> 7 mo.			1.9
1980	$138,300	↑	↑	↑	$164,400				↑	$149,600	↑	↓	2.7
1981	<9%> 15 mo.										↓		6.2
1982	↑	↑	↑	↑	+62% 28 mo.		↑	↑	↑	↑	↑	↑	32.6
1983	↑	↑	↑	↑	↑	↓	↓	↑	↑	↑	↑	↑	8.4
1984	$242,600	<5%> 4 mo.		$230,800		↑	↑	↑	↑	↑	↑	↑	15.1
1985	↑	↓	↑	↑	↑	↑	↓	↑	↑	↑	↑	↑	22.1
1986	↑	↑	↑	↑	+70% 33 mo.		↑	↑	↑	↑	↑	↑	15.3
1987	↑	$393,400	<5%> 7 mo.					$374,100	↑	↑	↑		2.8
1988	↑	↑	↓	↓	↓	↑	↑	↑	↑	↑	↓	↑	7.9
1989	↑	↑	↑	↑	↑	↑	↑	↓	↑	↑	↑	↑	14.5
1990	↓	↑	↑	↓	↑	↑	↑	↓	↑	↑	↑	↑	9.0
1991	↑	↑	↑	↑	+97% 76 mo.		↑	↑	↑	↑	↑	↑	16.0
1992	↓	↓	↓	↑	↑	↑	↑	↑	↑	↓	↓	↑	7.4
1993	↑	↑	↑	↑	↑	↑	↑	↑	↑	↑	↓	↑	9.7
1994	$738,500	<5%> 5 mo.			$700,500	↑	↑	↓	↓	↓	↓		-2.9
1995	↑	↑	↑	↑	↑	↑	↓	↑	↑	↑	↑	↑	18.5
1996	↑	↓	↓	↓	↑	↑	↑	↓	↑	↑	↑	↓	3.6
1997	↑	↑	↓	↑	↑	↑	↑	↓	↑	↑	↑	↑	9.7
1998	↑	↓	↑	↑	↑	↑	↑	↑	↑	↓	↑	↓	8.7
1999	↑	↓	↑	↑	↓	↓	↓	↓	↑	↑	↓	↓	-0.8
2000	↓	↑	↑	↓	↓	↑	↑	↑	↑	↑	↑	↑	11.6
2001	↑	↑	↑	↓	↓	+148% 165 mo.		↑	↑	↑	↓	↓	8.4
2002	↑	↑	↓	↑	↑	↑	↑	↑	↑	↓	↑	↑	10.3
2003	↑	↑	↓	↑	↑	↓	↓	↑	↑	↓	↑	↑	4.1
2004	↑	↑	↑	↓	↓	↑	↑	↑	↑	↑	↓	↑	4.3
2005	↑	↓	↓	↑	↑	↑	↓	↑	↓	↓	↑	↑	2.4
2006	↑	↑	↓	↓	↓	↑	↑	↑	↑	↑	↑	↓	4.3
2007	↓	↑	↑	↑	↓	↓	↑	↑	↑	↑	↑	↑	7.0
2008	↑	$1,738,300	<4%> 7 mo.					$1,671,700	↑	↑			5.2
2009	↓	↓	↑	↑	↑	↑	↑	↑	↑	↑	↑	↓	5.9
2010	↑	↑	↓	↑	+30% 38 mo.		↑	↑	↑	↓	↓	↓	6.5
2011	↑	↑	↑	↑	↑	↓	↑	↑	↑	↑	↓	$2,179,300	7.8%

Total Return: Includes dividends, interest and capital gains reinvested   **Standard Deviation: 6.7**

Source: Morningstar Direct: 50% SBBI LT Corp Index & 50% SBBI IT Govt Index (1972-1975); 100% Barcap US Aggregate Bond Index (1976-2011)

↑ ↓ *Up or Down Month*   ⬤ *Cyclical Declines*   ⬭ *Recovery (to pre-decline level)*   ◯ *Net New Advancement*

REWARD*		RISK PROFILE	
Average Annual Return (1972-2011)	8.0%	Average Bear Market Decline	<7%>
Riskless Return (T-bills)	<5.4%>	Worst Bear Market Decline	<13%>
AVERAGE ANNUAL REWARD OF BONDS	**2.6%**	*$100,000 held in U.S. Treasury bills over this time period grew to $825,900.*	

Annualized   ©2012 by Tanglewood Wealth Management, Inc.

CHART 7-4

International Stocks
Growth of $100,000
(12/31/71 – 12/31/11)

Year	Jan	Feb	Mar	Apr	May	Jun	Jul	Aug	Sep	Oct	Nov	Dec	Annual Returns
1972	$100,000	↑	↑	↑	+51% 15 mo.		↑	↑	↓	↑	↑	↑	36.3%
1973	↑	↑	$150,800		<42%> 18 mo.								-14.9
1974									$86,800	↑	↑	↓	-23.2
1975	↑	↑	↓	↑	↓	↓	↓	↑	↓	↑	↑	↑	35.4
1976	↑	↑	↓	↑	↓	↓	↓	↓	↑	↑	↑	↑	2.5
1977	↓	↑	↑	↑	↓	↑	↓	↓	↑	↑	↓	↑	18.1
1978	↑	↑	↑	↓	+196% 79 mo.		↑	↑	↑	↑	↓	↑	32.6
1979	↑	↓	↑	↓	↓	↑	↑	↑	↑	↓	↑	↑	4.8
1980	↑	↓	↓	↑	↑	↑	↑	↑	↑	↑	↓	↑	22.6
1981	↓	↓	↑	$256,600		<20%> 17 mo.				↑	↑	↑	-2.3
1982									$204,100	↑	↑	↑	-1.9
1983	↓	↑	↑	↑	+67% 18 mo.	↑	↑	↑	↑	↑	↑	↑	23.7
1984	↑	↑	$340,100	<17%> 4 mo.		$280,800	↑	↓	↑	↑	↑	↑	7.4
1985	↑	↓	↓	↓	↑	↑	↑	↑	↑	↑	↑	↑	56.2
1986	↑	↑	↑	↑	+323% 37 mo.	↑	↑	↑	↑	↑	↑	↑	69.4
1987	↑	↑	↑	↑	↓	↓	$1,187,500	<15%> 2 mo.		↑	↑		24.6
1988	↑	↑	↑	↑	+47% 26 mo.	↑	↓	↑	↑	↑	↓	↑	28.3
1989	↑	↑	↓	↓	↓	↑	↑	↓	↑	↓	$1,481,700		10.5
1990					<31%> 9 mo.				$1,026,200	↑	↑	↑	-23.4
1991	↑	↓	↓	↑	↑	↓	↑	↓	↑	↓	↓	↑	12.1
1992	↓	↓	↓	↑	↑	↓	↓	↑	↓	↓	↑	↑	-12.2
1993	↓	↑	↑	↑	↑	↑	↑	↑	↓	↑	↓	↑	32.6
1994	↑	↓	↓	↑	+112% 91 mo.	↑	↑	↑	↓	↑	↓	↑	8.3
1995	↓	↓	↑	↑	↓	↑	↑	↓	↑	↓	↑	↑	10.2
1996	↑	↑	↑	↑	↑	↓	↓	↑	↑	↓	↑	↓	6.5
1997	↓	↑	↓	↑	↑	↑	↑	↓	↑	↓	↑	↓	0.8
1998	↑	↑	↑	$2,175,500	<16%> 5 mo.				$1,820,000	↑	↑	↑	15.6
1999	↓	↓	↑	↑	+60% 15 mo.	↑	↑	↑	↑	↑	$2,907,600		32.6
2000					<45%> 33 mo.								-14.3
2001													-19.7
2002									$1,597,600	↑	↑	↓	-14.3
2003	↓	↓	↓	↑	↑	↑	↑	↑	↑	↑	↑	↑	41.6
2004	↑	↑	↑	↓	↓	↑	↓	↑	↑	↑	↑	↑	21.7
2005	↓	↑	↓	↓	+248% 61 mo.	↑	↑	↑	↑	↓	↑	↑	17.3
2006	↑	↓	↑	↑	↓	↓	↑	↑	↑	↑	↑	↑	28.1
2007	↑	↑	↑	↑	↑	↑	↓	↓	↑	$5,558,900			18.2
2008					<57%> 16 mo.								-45.3
2009		$2,374,200	↑	↑	↑	↓	↓	↑	↑	↓	↑	↑	43.3
2010	↓	↓	↑	↓	↓	↑	↑	↓	↑	↑	↓	↑	11.9
2011	↑	↑	↑	↑	↓	↓	↓	↓	↓	↑	↓	$3,980,400	-13.5%

Total Return: Includes reinvested dividends and capital gains   **Standard Deviation: 23.5**

Source: Morningstar Direct: 100% MSCI EAFE Index (1972-1993); 100% FTSE All World ex US Index (1994-2011)

↑ ↓ *Up or Down Month*   ⬤ *Cyclical Declines*   ⬭ *Recovery (to pre-decline level)*   ⬭ *Net New Advancement*

REWARD*		**RISK PROFILE**	
Average Annual Return (1972-2011)	9.6%	Average Bear Market Decline	<30%>
Riskless Return (T-bills)	< 5.4%>	Worst Bear Market Decline	<57%>
AVERAGE ANNUAL REWARD OF INTERNATIONAL MARKETS	**4.2%**	*$100,000 held in U.S. Treasury bills over this time period grew to $825,900.*	

*Annualized. ©2012 by Tanglewood Capital Management, Inc.

CHART 7-5

Equity REITs
Growth of $100,000
(12/31/71 – 12/31/11)

Year	Jan	Feb	Mar	Apr	May	Jun	Jul	Aug	Sep	Oct	Nov	Dec	Annual Returns
1972	$100,000 ↑	↓		+14% 9 mo.		↑	↑	↓	$113,800				8.0%
1973						<37%> 27 mo.							-15.5
1974												$71,700	-21.4
1975	↑	↑	↑	↑	↑	↑	↓	↓	↓	↓	↑	↑	19.3
1976	↑	↑	↑	↑	↑	↑	↑	↑	↑	↑	↑	↑	47.6
1977	↑	↑	↑	↑	↑	+246% 56 mo.		↑	↑	→	↑	↑	22.4
1978	↓	↑	↑	↑	↓	↑	↑	↑	↓	↓	↑	↑	10.3
1979	↑	↑	↑	↑	↓	↓	↑	$248,300	<13%> 2 mo.		↑	↑	35.9
1980	↑	↑	↓	↓	↑	↑	↑	↑	↓	↑	↓	↓	24.4
1981	↑	↑	↑	↑	↓	↑	↓	↓	↓	↑	↑	↓	6.0
1982	↓	↓	↓	↑	↓	↓	↑	↑	↑	↑	↑	↑	21.6
1983	↑	↓	↑	↑	↑	+324% 93 mo.		↑	↑	↑	↑	↑	30.6
1984	↑	↑	↑	↑	→	↓	↑	↑	↑	↑	↑	↑	20.9
1985	↑	↑	↑	↑	↑	↑	↓	↓	↑	↑	↑	↑	19.1
1986	↑	↑	↑	↓	↓	↑	↓	↑	↓	↑	↓	↓	19.2
1987	↑	↑	↑	↓	↓	↑	$919,700	<18%> 3 mo.	$755,100	↑	↑		-3.7
1988	↑	↑	↑	↑	↑	↑	↓	↓	↑	↑	↓	↑	13.5
1989	↑	↓	↑	↑	+37% 22 mo.		↑	$1,032,400	<24%> 14 mo.				8.8
1990						↑	↓	↓	$785,900	↑	↓		-15.3
1991	↑	↑	↑	↑	↑	↓	↑	↑	↓	↓	↓	↑	35.7
1992	↑	↓	↓	↓	↑	+115% 35 mo.		↑	↑	↓	↑	↑	14.6
1993	↑	↑	↑	↓	↓	↑	↑	↑	$1,685,800	<11%> 14 mo.			19.7
1994										$1,501,200	↑		3.2
1995	↓	↑	↓	↓	↑	↑	↑	↑	↑	↓	↑	↑	15.3
1996	↑	↑	↓	↑	↑	+101% 37 mo.		↑	↑	↑	↑	↑	35.3
1997	↑	↓	↓	↓	↑	↑	↑	↓	↑	↓	↑	$3,020,400	20.3
1998	↑					<24%> 23 mo.							-17.5
1999										$2,303,300	↑		-4.6
2000	↑	↓	↑	↑	↑	↑	↑	↓	↑	↓	↑	↑	26.4
2001	↑	↓	↑	↑	↑	↑	↓	↑	↓	↓	↑	↑	13.9
2002	↑	↑	↑	↑	↑	+137% 52 mo.		↓	↓	↓	↑	↑	3.8
2003	↓	↑	↑	↑	↑	↑	↑	↑	↑	↑	↑	↑	37.1
2004	↑		↑	$5,456,700	<15%>	↑	↑	↑	↓	↑	↑	↑	31.6
2005	↓	↓	↓	↑	↑	+127% 33 mo.		↓	↓	↓	↑	↑	12.2
2006	↑	↑	↑	↑	↓	↑	↑	↑	↑	↑	↑	↓	35.0
2007	$10,529,300												-15.7
2008						<68%> 25mo.							-37.7
2009		$3,338,200	↑	↑	↑	↑	↑	↑	↑	↓	↑	↑	28.0
2010	↓	↑	↑	↑	↓	↓	↑	↓	↑	↑	↓	↑	28.0
2011	↑	↑	↓	↑	↑	↑	↑	↓	↓	↑	↓	$9,043,000	8.3%

Total Return: Includes reinvested dividends and capital gains   **Standard Deviation: 18.7**

Source: Morningstar Direct: FTSE Nareit Equity REITs

↑ ↓ Up or Down Month   ⬤ Cyclical Declines   ⬭ Recovery (to pre-decline level)   ◯ Net New Advancement

REWARD*		RISK PROFILE	
Average Annual Return (1972-2011)	11.9%	Average Bear Market Decline	<26%>
Riskless Return (T-bills)	<5.4%>	Worst Bear Market Decline	<68%>
AVERAGE ANNUAL REWARD OF EQUITY REITs STOCKS	**6.5%**	*$100,000 held in U.S. Treasury bills over this time period grew to $825,900.*	

Annualized. ©2012 by Tanglewood Capital Management, Inc.

CHART 7-6

Gold
Growth of $100,000
(12/31/71 – 12/31/11)

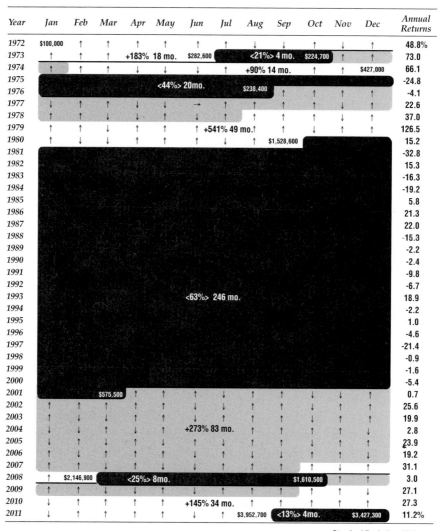

Year	Jan	Feb	Mar	Apr	May	Jun	Jul	Aug	Sep	Oct	Nov	Dec	Annual Returns
1972	$100,000	↑	↑	↑	↑	↑	↓	↓	↑	↓	↑		48.8%
1973	↑	↑	+183% 18 mo.		$282,600		<21%> 4 mo.		$224,700	↑	↑		73.0
1974	↑	↑	↑	↓	↓	↓	↑	+90% 14 mo.		↑	↑	$427,000	66.1
1975				<44%> 20mo.									-24.8
1976						$238,400		↑	↑	↑	↑	↑	-4.1
1977	↓	↑	↑	↓	↓	→	↑	↑	↑	↑	↑	↑	22.6
1978	↑	↑	↓	↓	↑	↓	↑	↑	↑	↑	↓	↑	37.0
1979	↑	↑	↓	↑	↑	↑	+541% 49 mo.		↑	↓	↑	↑	126.5
1980	↑	↓	↓	↑	↑	↑	↓	↑	$1,528,600				15.2
1981													-32.8
1982													15.3
1983													-16.3
1984													-19.2
1985													5.8
1986													21.3
1987													22.0
1988													-15.3
1989													-2.2
1990													-2.4
1991													-9.8
1992													-6.7
1993					<63%> 246 mo.								18.9
1994													-2.2
1995													1.0
1996													-4.6
1997													-21.4
1998													-0.9
1999													-1.6
2000													-5.4
2001				$575,500	↑	↑	↑	↓	↑	↑	↓	↓	↑	0.7
2002	↑	↑	↑	↓	↑	↓	↓	↑	↑	↓	↓	↑	25.6
2003	↑	↓	↓	↑	↑	↓	↑	↑	↑	↑	↑	↑	19.9
2004	↓	↓	↑	↓	+273% 83 mo.		↑	↑	↑	↑	↑	↓	2.8
2005	↓	↑	↓	↓	↓	↑	↓	↑	↑	↑	↑	↑	23.9
2006	↑	↓	↑	↑	↑	↓	↑	↓	↓	↑	↑	↓	19.2
2007	↑	↑	↓	↓	↓	↓	↑	↑	↑	↑	↓	↑	31.1
2008	↑	$2,146,900	<25%> 8mo.							$1,610,500	↑	↑	3.0
2009	↑	↑	↓	↑	↑	↓	↑	↑	↑	↑	↑	↓	27.1
2010	↓	↑	↑	↑	↑	+145% 34 mo.		↑	↑	↑	↑	↑	27.3
2011	↓	↑	↑	↑	↑	↓	↑	$3,952,700	<13%> 4mo.		$3,427,300		11.2%

Standard Deviation: 29.3

Source: Standard & Poor's Statistical Service, Metals Supplement 1972-2006; SPDR Gold ETF 2007-2011

↑ ↓ *Up or Down Month*   ▬ *Cyclical Declines*   ▬ *Recovery (to pre-decline level)*   ◯ *Net New Advancement*

REWARD*

Average Annual Return (1972-2011)	9.2%
Riskless Return (T-bills)	<5.4%>
AVERAGE ANNUAL REWARD OF GOLD	**3.8%**

RISK PROFILE

Average Bear Market Decline	<33%>
Worst Bear Market Decline	<63%>

$100,000 held in U.S. Treasury bills over this time period grew to $825,900.

Annualized ©2012 by Tanglewood Capital Management, Inc.

CHART 7-7

Asset Classes – Comparing Risks and Rewards

(1972-2011)

	Cash (30-Day T-Bills)	Bonds (5-Year Treasuries)	Bonds (Total U.S. Bonds)
REWARD			
Return (Annualized)	5.4%	7.5%	8.0%
Riskless Return (T-bills)	-5.4%	-5.4%	-5.4%
REWARD	**0%**	**2.1%**	**2.6%**
RISK PROFILE			
Worst Bear Market	0	<9%>	<13%>
Average Bear Market	0	<6%>	<7%>

	Total U.S. Stock Market	International Stocks (U.S. $)	Equity REITs	Gold
REWARD				
Return (Annualized)	9.8%	9.6%	11.9%	9.2%
Riskless Return (T-bills)	-5.4%	-5.4%	-5.4%	-5.4%
REWARD	**4.4%**	**4.2%**	**6.5%**	**3.8%**
RISK PROFILE				
Worst Bear Market	<51%>	<57%>	<68%>	<63%>
Average Bear Market	<31%>	<30%>	<26%>	<33%>

CHART 7-8

Evaluating the Asset Classes

A primary goal of this book is to develop the best portfolios built from history's top-performing asset classes. Charts 7-2 through 7-7 distill 40 years of head-to-head competition among these candidates for your Wealth and Retirement Portfolio. It shows the reward each provided and the risk endured to achieve that reward. The results are quite revealing.

It has long been observed that an investor must take more risk in order to achieve higher returns. Chart 7-8 clearly validates that observation.

Every asset class delivered a reward greater than the riskless rate (U.S. treasury bills) over its history. Yet each asset class also experienced varying degrees of bear market declines along the way.

Importantly, with the exception of gold, the rewards and risks were more or less *proportional*. The reward of U.S. Treasury bonds (5-year maturity) was the smallest of these asset classes – but so were its risks. The reward of the total U.S. bond market was moderately higher as were its risks.

Stocks, REITs and gold produced much higher returns but with much higher risks. The overall risks and returns of the U.S. stock market are very similar to those of international stocks – although there are variations in the timing and/or intensity of individual bear market declines within each.

REITs delivered the highest return between all these major asset classes between 1972 and 2011. Yet REITs also experienced the single largest bear market.

The bottom line is that there is no perfect asset class, one that offers *both* superior returns and low risks.

Each Asset Class is Its Own "Market"

Market commentators often refer to "the market cycle" as if all asset classes were following the same ebb and flow. As you look through the Historical Risk/Reward charts for each asset class within this chapter, take special notice of *when* their bear markets occurred. You will quickly notice that *there is no general market cycle.* At times, each asset class marches to its own drummer; each asset class is in effect a market unto itself.

 Certainly periods like 1973-'74 and 2007-'09 caught all of the common stock asset classes in their down draft, but not bonds or cash. Over the balance of the past 40 years, each asset class more or less advanced and declined in its own unique rhythm. Therefore, the performance of any investment such as a mutual fund, can only be fairly judged against the overall performance of the asset class within which it invests. For example, it would not be fair to judge the performance of an international stock fund by the performance of the S&P 500 index.

Conclusions

A primary goal of this book has been to develop an approach for wealth preservation that will preserve and enhance wealth even in uncertain investment climates. As is now clear, every asset class has rewarded its holders with a long-term return that is higher than the riskless rate of treasury bills. However, this excess return is earned as the investor must experience a poor investment environment with some unpredictable regularity. Fortunately, the bear market declines have always been fully recovered in the following bull market. There is little that is unique about the financial crisis period in this respect.

One other piece of good news is that the bear markets of the various asset classes do not perfectly align themselves. This creates an enormous opportunity for portfolio construction.

We are now ready to build consistent and predictable Wealth and Retirement Portfolios (of varying risk/reward characteristics) employing the following asset classes.

- 30-Day U.S. Treasury Bills
- 5-Year U.S. Treasury Bonds
- Total Domestic Bond Market

- **Total Domestic Stock Market**
- **International Stocks in U.S. Dollars**
- **Equity REITs**
- **Gold**

Any long term investor should find these asset classes to be worthy building blocks for a Wealth and Retirement Portfolio.

Section III

Asset Allocation Policies

and Model Portfolios

Overview of Section III

This section will take a thorough look at the impact of a portfolio's "asset allocation."

This term is used to denote the proportions of individual asset classes within a portfolio. The asset allocation of a well-diversified portfolio is the major determinant of its risks and rewards over the long term.

Maintaining relatively fixed allocations to reliable asset classes is the most predictable policy for long-term portfolio planning. Four high-performing asset allocations (Model Portfolios) covering four widely different levels of risk are introduced and thoroughly evaluated in this section.

Special attention was given to:

- How each asset allocation policy (Model Portfolio) performed during stressful market conditions such as the Great Depression and Financial Crisis

- What range of returns each offered during short and intermediate-term investment horizons

- How much income each could provide for a long retirement without threatening to run out prematurely

The Horserace and the "No Brainer"

One aspect of asset allocation is critical to understand. Investing is like a never-ending horserace with every asset class in the race. At any point in time, one or more asset classes will be leading the race and thereby driving your portfolio returns. (Later, those investments will fall back in the pack and others will lead for a while.) After a period of time, whichever investments are currently in the lead begin to feel like the <u>only</u> investment to own. Financial books and articles, as well as friends and associates, begin to refer to the leading asset class as a *"no brainer"*...as if it were destined to always beat the competition.

We've seen this so many times over the past few decades:

- The Nifty-Fifty growth stocks in the early '70s.
- Oil and gas in the mid-'70s.
- Real estate in the late '70s.
- Small stocks in the early '80s.
- Large stocks in the mid-'80s.
- Japanese (international) stocks in the late '80s.
- Emerging market stocks in the early '90s.
- S&P 500 stocks in the second half of the '90s.
- Residential homes in the early to mid-2000s.
- Emerging Markets in the mid to late 2000s.

Every single one of these examples shares these two characteristics: The noted asset class dominated other asset classes for a period of time, typically 2-4 years and then it dropped sharply and *severely underperformed* most other asset classes in the years following its leadership.

To preserve wealth overtime, it is critical to avoid concentration in the current winners as their leadership will come to an end....unexpectedly....just when everything seems to be going their way. *Diversifying across multiple asset classes has been the most stable, predictable wealth preservation strategy over time* which is one of the central messages of this book. This approach has been thoroughly vindicated in the uncertain post 2000 period despite the two major bear markets (2000-2002 and 2007-2009).

8

Creating Predictable
Long-Term Portfolios

Introduction

Substantially all of the investments within your Wealth and Retirement Portfolio can be placed in one of the seven major asset classes that survived close evaluation in Section II (including money market "cash" investments). The normal proportion that your portfolio holds of each major asset class is referred to as its *asset allocation.*

Your asset allocation will likely be the single largest contributor to your investment performance. An appropriate asset allocation policy offers the highest probability of achieving a targeted long-term rate of return and the least risk of falling short of your ultimate retirement objective.

Asset allocations have stood the test of time – through all of the good and bad markets of the past – including the poor and uncertain markets since 2000.

"As a football coach, I play not my 11 best but my best 11."

-Knute Rockne

Fundamental Principles

An asset allocation policy sets the proportions for each asset class held within a portfolio. Underlying the importance of such a policy are these fundamental principles:

- *Financial History is Rational and Repetitive (Over the Long-Term)* - The variation in returns from each asset class diminishes significantly with time. The longer an asset class (or combination of asset classes) is held, the more reliable its performance in relation to historical averages.

- *Primary Determinant of Performance* - The lion's share of a portfolio's long-term performance is determined by its asset allocation; the much smaller share is due to individual security selection. (Ironically, many investors approach the investment process as if the exact opposite were true.)

- *Diversification* - A cross-section of securities within an asset class is required in order to deliver the return associated with that asset class while minimizing the risk of opportunity loss (substantial underperformance).

Asset Allocation Policy

An asset allocation policy allocates a specific percentage of the total portfolio to each of the major asset classes: U.S. stocks, international stocks, REITs, U.S. Treasury bonds, U.S. total bond market, gold and cash.

An asset allocation policy establishes a highly desirable mix of asset classes that can be adhered to over time. Both the selection of asset classes to include and the weighting of each within the portfolio's asset allocation are critical to achieving success. Evaluating asset allocation strategies will be the focus of the remainder of this section. At a minimum, evaluating the risks and rewards of stable allocation strategies over long time periods provides a unique opportunity to uncover outstanding "benchmark portfolios." These are portfolios that have provided superior performance *without* the aid of human (or computer) changes over time other than periodic rebalancing.

Example of an asset allocation strategy:

Investment Policy	*Asset Allocation*
Stocks (45%)	30% dedicated to domestic mutual funds/ETFs 15% dedicated to International Stock mutual fund/ETFs
REITs (5%)	5% dedicated to equity REIT mutual funds/ETFs
Bonds (30%)	15% dedicated to Intermediate U.S. Treasury Bond mutual funds/ETFs 15% dedicated to Total U.S. Bond mutual funds/ETFs
Gold (5%)	5% 5% dedicated to gold bullion/ETFs
Cash (15%)	15% allocated to a general Money Market account
	100% Total Portfolio

CHART 8-1

An asset allocation policy such as this one provides a highly predictable track for your Wealth and Retirement Portfolio. The lion's share of its ultimate performance will be determined by strict adherence to the policy - regardless of the mutual funds, ETFs or individual stocks and bonds purchased for each asset class.

The point cannot be overemphasized that the selection of asset classes and the proportions decided upon are the primary determinant of any portfolio's final performance. *This is by far the most significant set of decisions with regard to your Wealth and Retirement Portfolio and/or its benchmark.*

For those who choose to invest via an asset allocation policy, their investment decisions become very focused. Mutual funds or ETFs are only evaluated against other mutual funds within the same asset class. For example, a domestic stock fund is only evaluated against other U.S. stock funds or an index of the U.S. stock market to fulfill that requirement of the asset allocation. (Strategies for evaluating and selecting mutual funds are thoroughly analyzed in Section IV.)

It should be readily apparent that you would not choose an asset allocation strategy unless you were completely committed to it.

Conclusion

Asset Allocation has replaced the fuzzier concept of diversification in providing discipline to portfolio investing. An appropriately developed asset allocation policy is the best structure for your Wealth and Retirement Portfolio.

9

Superior Portfolios
Well-Suited For
Uncertain Times

Introduction

Superior asset allocation policies combine asset classes so that the overall portfolio produces a high long-term reward relative to a specific level of risk (bear market declines).

Hundreds of combinations of the reliable asset classes (from Section II) have been evaluated in order to uncover historically high-performing asset allocation policies. Based upon these studies, four Model Portfolios are introduced.

The risk profiles of these Model Portfolios range from conservative to aggressive. Each of these Model Portfolios offers the prospect of long-term predictability for your Wealth and Retirement Portfolio even in the face of poor or uncertain market environments.

"Clients' expectations tend to err in an optimistic direction; they believe that higher returns are possible with less risk than is actually the case."

-Roger C. Gibson
Author of *Asset Allocation*, 1990

The Best Asset Allocation Strategy for You

The right asset allocation policy for you is the one that offers a high rate of return within *your* own comfort level for bear market declines (risk) - based on its long-term performance through all market conditions.

In order for you to isolate such an ideal portfolio structure, you should know the following information about any asset allocation policy you may be considering for your Wealth and Retirement Portfolio:

- the maximum decline it has suffered in a major bear market
- the range of declines it has incurred during normal cyclical bear markets
- the long-term *average return* it has delivered above that of 30-day Treasury bills (the riskless rate of return)
- the *range of returns* it has produced over various market conditions.

History is your best guide as to the risks and rewards that are inherent within complete portfolios just as it was with individual asset classes. Seeing is believing.

The outstanding asset allocation policies will now be introduced. These "Model Portfolios" should prove invaluable as you consider the best structure for your own portfolio or as a benchmark to measure your portfolio against.

Of course, you can still opt for the most common strategy - none at all. This is the hodge-podge portfolio discussed in Chapter 1 that never establishes nor adheres to a definite overall game plan and whose risks and rewards are all but unknown. Assuming you establish and adhere to an asset allocation policy, you will build a much higher level of predictability into your long-term planning.

Balanced Asset Allocation Policies & Correlation Benefits

 The term "balanced" is an excellent descriptive term for portfolios made up of stocks, bonds, real estate (REITs), gold and cash in that they bring together the growth from stocks, the inflation protected income of real estate (REITs), the higher income from bonds, the special security of gold and the ready liquidity and stability of cash equivalents.

As illustrated in Section II, the degrees of fluctuation are far different within these asset classes. As was pointed out in Chapter 7, the *direction* of advances or declines within one asset class may not correlate with those of another. Bonds may *zig* when stocks *zag*. This was clearly evident in the financial crisis and stock market meltdown of 2007-2009. High quality bonds went up in value as stocks went down. Cash was, of course, stable in market value. Asset classes that do not move up and down together are said to be uncorrelated.

By combining uncorrelated asset classes within your portfolio, you achieve the diversification necessary to smooth fluctuations and reduce overall risk. Academic research has proved that the more uncorrelated the returns from various asset classes, the less volatile will be the aggregate performance of a portfolio.

In addition, balanced asset allocations can lessen volatility for the same return. This is illustrated below by comparing the performance of the S&P 500 total return index with that of a balanced portfolio (66% stocks, 29% bonds, 5% gold, 4% cash) for the period from 1972 to 2011. (See Chart 9-1)

| | Comparison Period (1972-2011) | |
	Return	Worst Decline
S&P 500	9.8%	<51%>
Growth Balanced Portfolio*	9.9%	<36%>

Chart 9-1

*See Chart 9-6

 This is an excellent result - *a slightly higher return with far lower downside risk!* Not all balanced portfolios are created equal, however. Each specific portfolio design delivers unique long-term rewards and shorter-term risks.

Risk as Viewed from different viewpoints

Risk does not feel the same to every investor!

Model Portfolios

The Model Portfolios take advantage of the lack of correlation between asset classes. Three balanced portfolios: Conservative, Moderate, Growth and a 100% Stocks Model Portfolio are illustrated.

 Countless combinations of the seven participating asset classes were tested in order to uncover the asset allocation policy that produced a high and stable reward relative to its level of risk.

Each asset-allocation was rebalanced at the end of each calendar year, selling some of that year's asset class winners and using the proceeds to buy more of that year's asset class losers to bring the portfolio back into alignment with its asset allocation policy.

A requirement for each model portfolio is that it be meaningful and realistic for the specific group of investors for whom it is intended. Put simply, this means an asset allocation policy that refers to itself as "conservative" should have delivered a very low risk profile over its long history, yet still produced a reward that finances a much higher level of retirement income than a straight bond and/or cash portfolio. The terms "moderate" and "growth" should also meet similar tests when slotted into the full historic range of risks and rewards.

 The following four Model Portfolios are proven combinations of all seven qualifying asset classes. These Model Portfolios have offered very high rewards for their respective levels of risk.

Conservative Balanced Portfolio

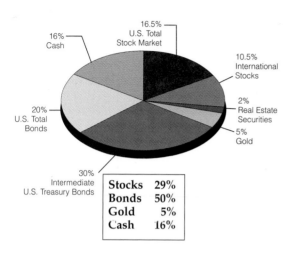

Stocks	29%
Bonds	50%
Gold	5%
Cash	16%

Primary Objective: The asset allocation that delivered a particularly high rate of return for a portfolio that did not sustain more than 25% of the bear market risk of stocks (the S&P 500 Index).

Performance Highlights: *(1972-2011)*

Rate of Return	8.7%
Riskless Rate (T-bills)	-5.4%
Reward	**3.3%**

Average Bear Market Decline: 7%

Worst Bear Market Decline: 12%

Moderate Balanced Portfolio

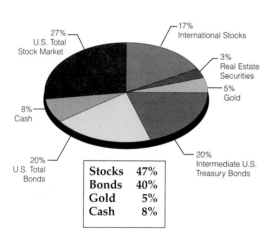

Stocks	47%
Bonds	40%
Gold	5%
Cash	8%

Primary Objective: The asset allocation that delivered a particularly high rate of return that did not sustain more than one-half of the bear market risk of stocks (the S&P 500 Index).

Performance Highlights: *(1972-2011)*

Rate of Return	9.4%
Riskless Rate (T-bills)	-5.4%
Reward	**4.0%**

Average Bear Market Decline: 12%

Worst Bear Market Decline: 23%

CHART 9-2

Growth Balanced Portfolio

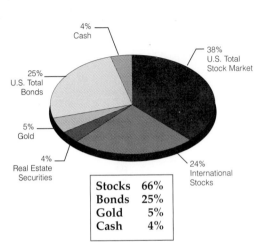

Stocks	66%
Bonds	25%
Gold	5%
Cash	4%

Primary Objective: The asset allocation that delivered a particularly high rate of return for a portfolio that did not sustain more than two-thirds of the bear market risk of stocks (the S&P 500 Index).

Performance Highlights: (1972-2011)

Rate of Return	10.0%
Riskless Rate (T-bills)	-5.4%
Reward	**4.6%**

Average Bear Market Decline: 18%
Worst Bear Market Decline: 36%

All Equity Portfolio

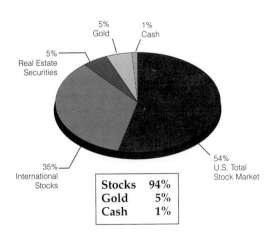

Stocks	94%
Gold	5%
Cash	1%

Primary Objective: The asset allocation that delivered a particularly high rate of return for a portfolio that did not sustain more bear market risk than that of the S&P 500 Index.

Performance Highlights: (1972-2011)

Rate of Return	10.4%
Riskless Rate (T-bills)	-5.4%
Reward	**5.0%**

Average Bear Market Decline: 27%
Worst Bear Market Decline: 51%

CHART 9-3

Excess Return from Rebalancing Uncorrelated Asset Classes

Balanced asset allocations generally provide higher long-term returns than the underlying asset classes. How is that possible... it sounds like 2 + 2 = 5?! It's made possible by rebalancing a portfolio of uncorrelated asset classes back to its fixed weightings on a periodic basis.

In calculating the historical performance of the Model Portfolios, each portfolio was rebalanced at the end of every calendar year to bring it back into alignment with its asset allocation policy. (As stated earlier, this is accomplished by selling the *excess* percentage weightings from his "winners" - from the year just ending - and adding the proceeds to those asset classes that underperformed and were therefore underweight in his portfolio at year end.)

 Rebalancing portfolios in this way produces an *additional* incremental rate of return. The *free* or enhanced returns for the balanced Model Portfolios from annual rebalancing in the 1972-2011 period were as follows:

Conservative Balanced	0.7% annually
Moderate Balanced	0.8% annually
Growth Balanced	0.8% annually

This is the difference between the actual compounded annual performance of these models (rebalanced annually) and simply adding up the individual compounded annual returns of the underlying asset classes (by their weighting within the model portfolio).

 For example, the Moderate Balanced Model delivered a 9.4% compounded rate of return during the 1972-2011 period, yet simply adding up the returns from the component asset classes during that same period (by their weighting within the portfolio) results in a total rate of return of just 8.6%.

Charts 9-4 through 9-7 are Historical Risk/Reward charts for the four Model Portfolios covering the period 1972-2011.

Conservative Balanced Portfolio*

Growth of $100,000
(12/31/71 – 12/31/11)

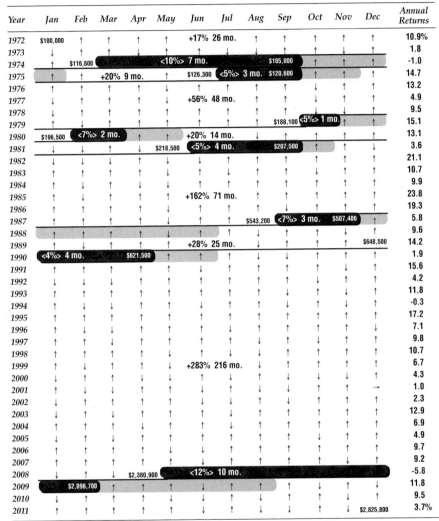

Year	Jan	Feb	Mar	Apr	May	Jun	Jul	Aug	Sep	Oct	Nov	Dec	Annual Returns
1972	$100,000					+17% 26 mo.							10.9%
1973													1.8
1974		$116,600		<10%> 7 mo.					$105,000				-1.0
1975			+20% 9 mo.			$126,300	<5%> 3 mo.	$120,600					14.7
1976													13.2
1977						+56% 48 mo.							4.9
1978													9.5
1979									$188,100	<5%> 1 mo.			15.1
1980	$196,500	<7%> 2 mo.				+20% 14 mo.							13.1
1981					$218,500	<5%> 4 mo.		$207,500					3.6
1982													21.1
1983													10.7
1984													9.9
1985						+162% 71 mo.							23.8
1986													19.3
1987								$543,200	<7%> 3 mo.		$507,400		5.8
1988													9.6
1989						+28% 25 mo.						$648,500	14.2
1990	<4%> 4 mo.			$621,500									1.9
1991													15.6
1992													4.2
1993													11.8
1994													-0.3
1995													17.2
1996													7.1
1997													9.8
1998													10.7
1999						+283% 216 mo.							6.7
2000													4.3
2001													1.0
2002													2.3
2003													12.9
2004													6.9
2005													4.9
2006													9.7
2007													9.2
2008				$2,380,900		<12%> 10 mo.							-5.8
2009	$2,096,700												11.8
2010													9.5
2011												$2,825,800	3.7%

Total Return: Includes dividends, interest and capital gains reinvested   Standard Deviation: 6.3

* 29% Stocks; 66% Fixed Income and Cash; 5% Gold. Asset Allocations (rebalanced annually): 16.5% to Domestic Stocks; 10.5% to International Stocks; 2% to Real Estate Securities; 5% Gold; 20% to U.S. Total Bonds; 30% to U.S. Treasuries; and 16% Cash.

↑ ↓ Up or Down Month   Cyclical Declines   Recovery (to pre-decline level)   Net New Advancement

REWARD**		RISK PROFILE	
Average Annual Return (1972-2011)	8.7%	Average Bear Market Decline	< 7%>
Riskless Return (T-bills)	<5.4%>	Worst Bear Market Decline	<12%>
AVERAGE ANNUAL REWARD OF CONSERVATIVE BALANCED PORTFOLIO	**3.3%**	$100,000 invested in U.S. Treasury bills over this time period grew to $825,900.	

**Annualized   ©2012 by Tanglewood Wealth Management, Inc.

CHART 9-4

Moderate Balanced Portfolio*

Growth of $100,000
(12/31/71 – 12/31/11)

Year	Jan	Feb	Mar	Apr	May	Jun	Jul	Aug	Sep	Oct	Nov	Dec	Annual Returns
1972	$100,000	↑	↑	↑	↑	+17% 22 mo.		↑	↓	↑	↑		14.4%
1973	↓	↑	↑	↑	↓	↑	↓	↓	↓	$117,400			-2.3
1974					<17%> 11 mo.				$97,400	↑	↑	↓	-6.9
1975	↑	↑		↑	↓	↓	↓	↓	↑	↑	↑	↑	20.0
1976	↑	↑	↑	↑	↓	+110% 64 mo.		↑	↑	↓	↑	↑	14.9
1977	↓	↑	↑	↓	↓	↓	↓	↓	↓	↓	↑	↑	5.5
1978	↓	↑	↑	↑	↑	↑	↑	↑	↓	↓	↓	↑	11.8
1979	↑	↓	↑	↑	↑	↑	↑	↑	↑	↓	↑	↑	17.0
1980	$204,800	<9%> 2 mo.		↓	↑	↑	↑	+25% 12 mo.		↑	↑	↓	16.7
1981	↓	↓	$232,400		<8%> 6 mo.			$214,900	↑	↓	↓	↓	1.1
1982	↓	↓	↓	↑	↓	↓	↑	↑	↑	↑	↑	↑	19.7
1983	↑	↑	↑	↑	↓	↑	↑	↑	↑	↓	↑	↑	13.7
1984	↑	↓	↑	↓	↓	↑	↓	↑	↑	↑	↑	↑	8.6
1985	↑	↓	↑	↑	↑	+200% 71 mo.		↑	↓	↑	↑	↑	28.3
1986	↑	↑	↑	↓	↓	↑	↓	↑	↓	↑	↑	↓	24.0
1987	↑	↑	↑	↑	↓	↑	↑	$645,100	↓	↓	$571,600	↑	7.0
1988	↑	↑	↑	↑	↓	↑	↓	↓	↑	↑	↓	↑	12.4
1989	↑	↓	↑	↑	↓	+34% 25 mo.		↓	↑	↓	$767,500	↓	16.1
1990					<7%> 9 mo.			$711,700		↑	↑	↑	-1.8
1991	↑	↑	↑	↑	↑	↓	↑	↑	↑	↑	↓	↑	18.4
1992	↓	↓	↓	↑	↑	↓	↑	↓	↑	↑	↑	↑	3.7
1993	↑	↑	↑	↑	↑	↑	↑	↑	↑	↑	↓	↑	14.1
1994	↑	↓	↓	↑	↑	↓	↑	↑	↓	↑	↓	↑	0.4
1995	↑	↑	↑	↑	+184% 119 mo.		↑	↑	↑	↓	↑	↑	19.7
1996	↑	↑	↑	↑	↑	↑	↓	↑	↑	↑	↑	↓	9.5
1997	↑	↑	↓	↑	↑	↑	↑	↓	↑	↓	↑	↑	12.2
1998	↑	↑	↑	↑	↓	↑	↓	↓	↑	↑	↑	↑	12.7
1999	↑	↓	↑	↑	↓	↑	↓	↑	↓	↑	↑	↑	10.8
2000	↓	↑	↑	↓	↓	↑	↓	$2,017,800	↓	↓	↓	↑	1.2
2001					<10%> 25 mo.								-2.4
2002								$1,812,100				↓	-2.2
2003	↓	↓	↑	↑	↑	↑	↓	↑	↑	↑	↑	↑	18.9
2004	↑	↑	↑	↓	↑	↑	↓	↑	↑	↑	↑	↑	9.5
2005	↓	↑	↓	↓	↑	+80% 61 mo.		↑	↑	↓	↑	↑	6.6
2006	↑	↑	↑	↑	↓	↑	↑	↑	↑	↑	↑	↓	12.9
2007	↑	↑	↑	↑	↑	↓	↑	↑	$3,264,800	↓	↓	↓	9.4
2008					<23%> 16 mo.								-14.6
2009		$2,500,800	↑	↑	↑	↑	↑	↑	↑	↑	↑	↑	18.0
2010	↓	↑	↑	↑	+53% 26 mo.		↓	↓	↑	↓	↓	↑	11.6
2011	↑	↑	↑	$3,821,200	<7%> 5 mo.			$3,544,600	↑	↓	$3,696,000		2.1%

Total Return: Includes dividends, interest and capital gains reinvested   **Standard Deviation: 9.0**

* 47% Stocks; 48% Fixed Income and Cash; 5% Gold. Asset Allocations (rebalanced annually): 27% to Domestic Stocks; 17% to International Stocks; 3% to Real Estate Securities; 5% to Gold; 20% to US Total Bonds; 20% US Treasuries; and 8% Cash.

↑ ↓ Up or Down Month   ● Cyclical Declines   ● Recovery (to pre-decline level)   ⬭ Net New Advancement

REWARD**

Average Annual Return (1972-2011)	9.4%
Riskless Return (T-bills)	< 5.4%>
AVERAGE ANNUAL REWARD OF MODERATE BALANCED PORTFOLIO	**4.0%**

RISK PROFILE

Average Bear Market Decline	<12%>
Worst Bear Market Decline	<23%>

$100,000 invested in U.S. Treasury bills over this time period grew to $825,900.

**Annualized ©2012 by Tanglewood Wealth Management, Inc.

CHART 9-5

Growth Balanced Portfolio*

Growth of $100,000
(12/31/71 – 12/31/11)

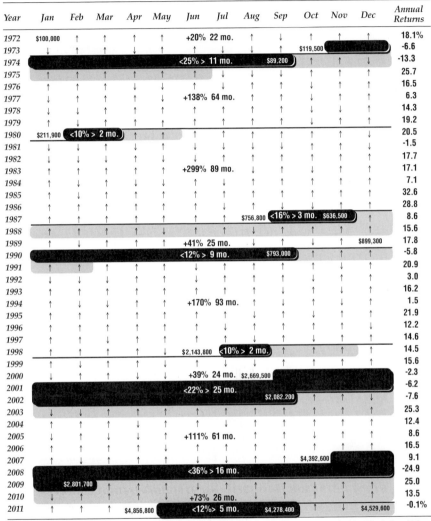

Year	Jan	Feb	Mar	Apr	May	Jun	Jul	Aug	Sep	Oct	Nov	Dec	Annual Returns
1972	$100,000	↑	↑	↑	↑	+20% 22 mo.		↑	↓	↑	↑	↑	18.1%
1973	↓	↓	↑	↓	↓	↓	↓	↓	$119,500				-6.6
1974					<25% > 11 mo.			$89,200		↑	↑	↓	-13.3
1975	↑	↑	↑	↑	↑	↓	↓	↑	↓	↑	↑	↑	25.7
1976	↑	↑	↑	↓	↓	↑	↓	↑	↑	↓	↑	↑	16.5
1977	↓	↑	↑	↑	↓	+138% 64 mo.		↑	↑	↓	↑	↑	6.3
1978	↓	↓	↑	↑	↑	↑	↑	↑	↓	↓	↓	↑	14.3
1979	↑	↓	↑	↑	↑	↑	↑	↑	↑	↓	↑	↑	19.2
1980	$211,900	<10% > 2 mo.		↑	↑	↑	↑	↑	↑	↑	↑	↓	20.5
1981	↓	↑	↑	↓	↓	↓	↓	↓	↓	↑	↑	↓	-1.5
1982	↓	↓	↓	↑	↓	↓	↑	↑	↑	↑	↑	↑	17.7
1983	↑	↑	↑	↑	↑	+299% 89 mo.		↓	↑	↓	↑	↑	17.1
1984	↑	↓	↑	↓	↓	↑	↓	↑	↑	↑	↓	↑	7.1
1985	↑	↑	↑	↑	↑	↑	↑	↑	↓	↑	↑	↑	32.6
1986	↑	↑	↑	↑	↑	↑	↓	↑	↓	↑	↑	↑	28.8
1987	↑	↑	↑	↑	↑	↑	↑	$756,800	<16% > 3 mo.	$636,500		↑	8.6
1988	↑	↑	↑	↑	↓	↑	↑	↓	↑	↑	↓	↑	15.6
1989	↑	↓	↑	↑	↑	+41% 25 mo.		↓	↑	↓	↑	$899,300	17.8
1990					<12% > 9 mo.			$793,000		↑	↑	↑	-5.8
1991	↑	↑	↑	↑	↑	↓	↑	↑	↑	↑	↓	↑	20.9
1992	↓	↓	↓	↑	↑	↓	↑	↓	↑	↓	↑	↑	3.0
1993	↑	↑	↑	↑	↑	↑	↑	↑	↓	↑	↓	↑	16.2
1994	↑	↓	↓	↑	+170% 93 mo.		↑	↑	↓	↑	↓	↑	1.5
1995	↑	↑	↑	↑	↑	↑	↑	↓	↑	↓	↑	↑	21.9
1996	↑	↑	↑	↑	↑	↑	↓	↑	↑	↑	↑	↓	12.2
1997	↑	↑	↓	↑	↑	↑	↑	↓	↑	↓	↑	↑	14.6
1998	↑	↑	↑	↑	↓	$2,143,800	<10% > 2 mo.	↑	↑	↑	↑	↑	14.5
1999	↑	↓	↑	↑	↓	↑	↓	↓	↓	↑	↑	↑	15.6
2000	↓	↑	↑	↓	+39% 24 mo.		$2,669,500						-2.3
2001					<22% > 25 mo.								-6.2
2002							$2,082,200		↑	↑	↓		-7.6
2003	↓	↓	↓	↑	↑	↑	↑	↑	↑	↑	↑	↑	25.3
2004	↑	↑	↓	↓	↑	↑	↓	↑	↑	↑	↑	↑	12.4
2005	↓	↑	↓	↓	+111% 61 mo.		↑	↑	↓	↑	↑	8.6
2006	↑	↑	↑	↑	↓	↑	↑	↑	↑	↑	↑	↑	16.5
2007	↑	↓	↑	↑	↑	↓	↓	↑	↑	$4,392,600			9.1
2008					<36% > 16 mo.								-24.9
2009		$2,801,700	↑	↑	↑	↑	↑	↑	↑	↓	↑	↑	25.0
2010	↑	↑	↓	↑	+73% 26 mo.		↓	↑	↑	↓	↓	↑	13.5
2011	↑	↑	↑	$4,856,800	<12%> 5 mo.		$4,278,400		↑	↓	$4,529,600	-0.1%

Total Return: Includes dividends, interest and capital gains reinvested   **Standard Deviation: 12.3**

* 66% Stocks; 29% Fixed Income and Cash; 5% Gold. Asset Allocations (rebalanced annually): 38% to Domestic Stocks; 24% to International Stocks; 4% to Real Estate Securities; 5% to Gold; 25% to U.S. Total Bonds; and 4% Cash.

↑ ↓ Up or Down Month　⬤ Cyclical Declines　　◯ Recovery (to pre-decline level)　◯ Net New Advancement

REWARD**		RISK PROFILE	
Average Annual Return (1972-2011)	10.0%	Average Bear Market Decline	<18%>
Riskless Return (T-bills)	< 5.4%>	Worst Bear Market Decline	<36%>
AVERAGE ANNUAL REWARD OF GROWTH BALANCED PORTFOLIO	**4.6%**	*$100,000 invested in U.S. Treasury bills over this time period grew to $825,900.*	

**Annualized* ©2012 by Tanglewood Wealth Management, Inc.

CHART 9-6

All Equity Portfolio*
Growth of $100,000
(12/31/71 – 12/31/11)

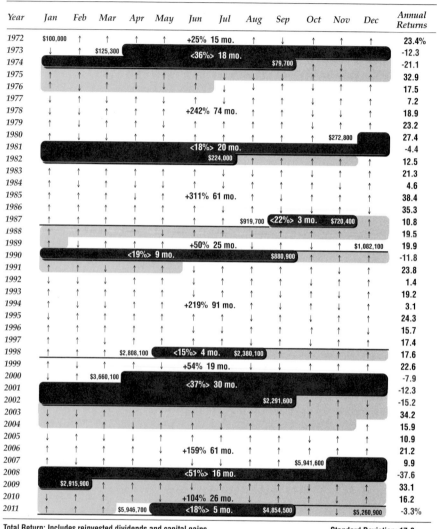

Year	Jan	Feb	Mar	Apr	May	Jun	Jul	Aug	Sep	Oct	Nov	Dec	Annual Returns
1972	$100,000	↑	↑	↑	↑	+25% 15 mo.		↑	↓	↑	↑	↑	23.4%
1973	↓	↑	$125,300			<36%> 18 mo.				↓			-12.3
1974									$79,700	↑	↓	↑	-21.1
1975	↑	↑	↑	↑	↑	↑	↑	↓	↑	↓	↑	↑	32.9
1976	↑	↓	↑	↓	↓	↑	↓	↓	↑	↓	↑	↑	17.5
1977	↓	↑	↓	↑	↓	↑	↓	↓	↑	↓	↑	↑	7.2
1978	↓	↓	↑	↑	↑	+242% 74 mo.		↑	↑	↓	↓	↑	18.9
1979	↑	↓	↑	↑	↓	↑	↑	↑	↑	↓	↑	↑	23.2
1980	↑	↓	↓	↑	↑	↑	↑	↑	↑	↑	$272,800		27.4
1981	↓	↑	↑	↑		<18%> 20 mo.			↑	↑	↑	↑	-4.4
1982						$224,000		↑	↑	↑	↑	↑	12.5
1983	↑	↑	↑	↑	↑	↑	↓	↑	↑	↓	↑	↑	21.3
1984	↑	↓	↑	↓	↓	↑	↓	↑	↑	↑	↓	↑	4.6
1985	↑	↑	↑	↓	↑	+311% 61 mo.		↑	↓	↑	↑	↑	38.4
1986	↑	↑	↑	↑	↑	↑	↓	↑	↓	↑	↑	↓	35.3
1987	↑	↑	↑	↑	↑	↑	↑	$919,700	<22%> 3 mo.	$720,400	↑	↓	10.8
1988	↑	↑	↑	↑	↓	↑	↓	↓	↑	↑	↓	↑	19.5
1989	↑	↓	↑	↑	↑	+50% 25 mo.		↓	↑	↓	↑	$1,082,100	19.9
1990	↑	↓	↑		<19%> 9 mo.				$880,900	↑	↑	↑	-11.8
1991	↑	↑	↓	↑	↑	↓	↑	↑	↓	↑	↓	↑	23.8
1992	↓	↓	↓	↑	↑	↓	↑	↓	↑	↓	↑	↑	1.4
1993	↑	↑	↑	↑	↑	↓	↑	↑	↓	↑	↓	↑	19.2
1994	↑	↓	↓	↑	↑	+219% 91 mo.		↑	↓	↑	↓	↑	3.1
1995	↓	↑	↑	↑	↑	↑	↑	↑	↑	↓	↑	↑	24.3
1996	↑	↑	↑	↑	↑	↑	↓	↑	↑	↑	↑	↓	15.7
1997	↑	↑	↓	↑	↑	↑	↑	↓	↑	↓	↑	↑	17.4
1998	↑	↑	↑	$2,808,100	<15%> 4 mo.		$2,380,100	↑	↑	↑	↑	↑	17.6
1999	↑	↓	↑	↑	↓	+54% 19 mo.		↓	↑	↓	↑	↑	22.6
2000	↓	↑	$3,660,100		<37%> 30 mo.								-7.9
2001													-12.3
2002								$2,291,600	↑	↑	↑	↓	-15.2
2003	↑	↑	↑	↑	↑	↑	↑	↑	↑	↑	↑	↑	34.2
2004	↑	↑	↑	↓	↑	↑	↓	↑	↑	↑	↑	↑	15.9
2005	↓	↑	↓	↓	↑	↑	↑	↓	↑	↓	↑	↑	10.9
2006	↑	↑	↑	↑	↓	+159% 61 mo.		↑	↑	↑	↑	↑	21.2
2007	↑	↓	↑	↑	↑	↓	↓	↑	$5,941,600				9.9
2008	↓		<51%> 16 mo.										-37.6
2009	$2,915,900	↑	↑	↑	↑	↑	↑	↑	↑	↓	↑	↑	33.1
2010	↑	↑	↑	↑	+104% 26 mo.		↑	↑	↑	↓	↑	↑	16.2
2011	↑	↑	↑	$5,946,700	<18%> 5 mo.		$4,854,500	↑	↓	$5,260,900			-3.3%

Total Return: Includes reinvested dividends and capital gains   **Standard Deviation: 17.0**

* *94% Stocks; 5% Gold; 1% Cash. Asset Allocations (rebalanced annually): 54% to Domestic Stocks; 35% to International Stocks; 5% to Real Estate Securities; 5% to Gold; and 1% Cash.*

↑ ↓ *Up or Down Month*   *Cyclical Declines*   *Recovery (to pre-decline level)*   *Net New Advancement*

REWARD**

Average Annual Return (1972-2011)	10.4%	
Riskless Return (T-bills)	< 5.4%>	
AVERAGE ANNUAL REWARD OF ALL EQUITY PORTFOLIO	**5.0%**	

RISK PROFILE

Average Bear Market Decline	<27%>
Worst Bear Market Decline	<51%>

$100,000 invested in U.S. Treasury bills over this time period grew to $825,900.

**Annualized* ©2012 by Tanglewood Wealth Management, Inc.

CHART 9-7

Evaluating the Model Portfolios

Rewards. The table below shows the cumulative return achieved by each model portfolio (and cash) during the 1972-2011 period from an initial investment of $100,000.

Model Portfolio Growth - $100,000 (1972-2011)

Cash (Treasury Bills)	Conservative Balanced	Moderate Balanced	Growth Balanced	All Equity (100% Stocks)
$825,900	$2,825,800	$3,696,000	$4,529,600	$5,260,900

The return from a Conservative Balanced portfolio more than tripled the return from T-bills. This is three times the principal, which provides three times the retirement income. A Moderate Balanced portfolio more than quadruples the return from cash, a Growth Balanced portfolio provides about five and a half times and 100% Stocks resulted in nearly six and a half times more principal and income-generating capacity.

The long-term rewards from these Model Portfolios have been very significant indeed! Chart 9-8 illustrates the total cumulative real returns from the four domestic model portfolios from 1972 through 2011 after adjusting for inflation. This is an excellent view of their wealth creation histories.

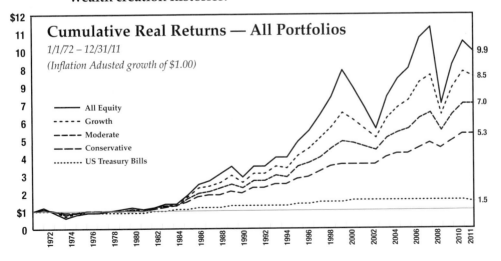

Cumulative Real Returns — All Portfolios
1/1/72 – 12/31/11
(Inflation Adusted growth of $1.00)

— All Equity
- - - - - Growth
— — Moderate
— — Conservative
.... US Treasury Bills

CHART 9-8

Another view of the performance of the Conservative Balanced portfolio is to compare its reward (return above T-bills) with those of portfolios made up of only bonds, 5-year Treasury bonds or the Total U.S. Bond Market in this example. (See Chart 9-9)

Performance Comparison: Conservative Balanced Model vs. Bonds - 1972-2011

	Reward*	Worst Decline	Average Decline
Conservative Balanced (Domestic Only)	3.3%	12%	7%
5-Year Treasury Bonds	2.1%	9%	6%
Total U.S. Bond Market	2.6%	13%	7%

*Reward is the total return *less* the return from cash (T-bills).

The Conservative model produced a significantly higher reward than bonds while not measurably increasing risk.

Chart 9-9

Risks.   The balanced Model Portfolios provide widely different answers to the question, "What's the worst that can happen?" There is certainly a wide variance in the temporary suffering of those choosing a Conservative Balanced Portfolio (12% worst bear market decline), a Moderate Balanced Portfolio (23%), and Growth Balanced Portfolio (36%).

The differences between these three Model Portfolios were far less pronounced when comparing their respective *average* bear market declines of 7%, 12% and 18%. *In other words, among the balanced Model Portfolios there is not nearly as significant a difference in normal bear market risk as would be suggested by their worst-case scenarios.*

Performance in Uncertain Times

As the title of this book suggests, it is important to establish an investment strategy that has worked – even in the overall poor market conditions that have persisted since the turn of the millennium in 2000.

So how did the Model Portfolios navigate this very tough terrain? Chart 9-10 provides the results.

Model Performance in the Uncertain Era

	Performance: 2000 – 2011	
	Annualized Return	Cumulative Return
Cash (30 day T-Bills)	2.3%	31%
Inflation	2.5%	34%
S&P 500 Index	0.6%	7%
All Equity Model Portfolio	3.3%	47%
Growth Model Portfolio	4.8%	75%
Moderate Model Portfolio	5.5%	90%
Conservative Model Portfolio	5.7%	95%

Source: Ibbotson SSB1, Charts 9-4 thru 9-7

Chart 9-10

As would be expected, the reward of equity ownership was far below its long-term average. Yet there was still a higher return than that of cash investments – for this obviously poor period. And the All Equity Portfolio vastly outperformed the highly regarded S&P 500 index. The three balanced portfolios performed even better, as would be expected in an era of extreme volatility. The Growth Portfolio posted an average annual reward of 2.5% (over Treasury bills) versus the long-term average of 4.6%. This was a solid performance for this period.

However, it is the Moderate and Conservative Model Portfolios experience in this period that deserve real attention. The Moderate Portfolio's 3.2% annualized reward (over T-bills) was not that far off its long-term average of 4.0%. This is an excellent performance for such an uncertain environment. The Conservative Portfolios performance is remarkable. Its annualized reward of 3.4% (over T-bills) was actually just above its long-term average of 3.3%.

The four Model Portfolios introduced in this chapter certainly delivered more than respectable results – even in this era of volatility and poor market conditions.

By closely evaluating each model portfolio, you are miles ahead of most investors in appreciating the inherent risks and rewards of the best asset allocation policies.

Note: All of the results of the portfolios presented in this chapter may be duplicated using the databases cited in Chart 7-1.

Comparing the Model Portfolios to each other brings the risk/reward relationship into clear view once again. An investor in a Balanced Conservative portfolio earned an annualized reward of 3.3% over U.S. Treasury bills for which the investor experienced a decline in his portfolio value of 7% (on average) approximately once every five years. An investor in a Balanced Moderate portfolio provided an annualized reward (total return less the return from T-bills) of 4.0% for which the investor had to endure a 13% decline in his portfolio value about twice per decade.

A Balanced Growth portfolio delivered a reward of 4.6% but suffered through cyclical bear markets averaging 18%. An All Equity Model Portfolio Investor enjoyed an average annual reward of 5.0%, while having to see 27% of his portfolio temporarily disappear (on average) about once every five years before being fully recovered in the following bull market.

Conclusion

Selecting and adhering to one of the Model Portfolios puts the wind at your back as you sail through the years with your Wealth and Retirement Portfolio. You have channeled the best information from the history of investing right into the structure of your portfolio. *You are selecting an asset allocation policy that delivered a very high historical reward for your comfortable level of risk.* You also have a thorough insight into the degree of volatility to which your own portfolio is exposed...*in advance.*

 Just how good are the Model Portfolios? Review the comparison in Chart 9-1. The S&P 500 is rightfully credited with outstanding long-term performance, yet the Balanced Growth portfolio with approximately 34% allocated to bonds, gold and cash provided a very similar return to the S&P 500 index over the 40 years between 1972 and 2011 with significantly reduced risk.

10

The Ultimate Period of Uncertainty: The Great Depression

Introduction

How would the Model Portfolios introduced in Chapter 9 have performed during the Great Depression? In order to answer this question, a different but similar set of Model Portfolios utilizing the data that was available in those years will be constructed.

Say you invested at the top of the market in 1929. You were convinced of the logic of disciplined strategy, so you stayed the course with one of the Model Portfolios throughout the Great Depression. What then?

Each *Depression Era Model Portfolio's* performance is examined in both nominal and real U.S. dollars through the full market cycle from 1929 through 1937 with interesting and counter-intuitive results.

> *"In the main, therefore, slumps are experiences to be lived through…with as much equanimity and patience as possible."*
>
> — John Maynard Keynes (1938)

What is your greatest *fear* when it comes to your investments? For many investors, a possible replay of the Great Depression tops the list. Therefore, a careful study of how Model Portfolios performed during that tragic period should be of great value.

Investors today have lived with uncertain politics, economics and markets. Yet nothing today compares to the enormous dislocations and uncertainty of the Great Depression. Thus, that era of "ultimate uncertainty" is very useful to today's investors in trying to understand……how bad could it get?

Simple Model Portfolios

Unfortunately, the Model Portfolios introduced in Chapter 9 cannot be used for this test for the following reasons:

- There is a lack of high quality data for international stocks in those years

- REITs were not invented until the 1960s

- Gold was illegal to own by individuals in those years

Therefore, we will construct purely domestic portfolios of stocks, bonds and cash that mimic the more diversified models from Chapter 9. These "Simple Model Portfolios" are shown in Chart 10-1.

Simple Conservative Portfolio

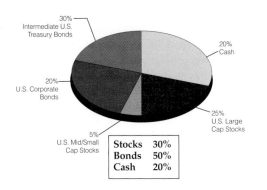

30%
Intermediate U.S.
Treasury Bonds

20%
Cash

20%
U.S. Corporate
Bonds

25%
U.S. Large
Cap Stocks

5%
U.S. Mid/Small
Cap Stocks

Stocks	30%
Bonds	50%
Cash	20%

Simple Growth Portfolio

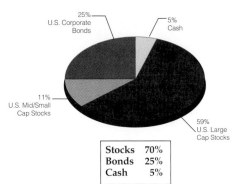

25%
U.S. Corporate
Bonds

5%
Cash

11%
U.S. Mid/Small
Cap Stocks

59%
U.S. Large
Cap Stocks

Stocks	70%
Bonds	25%
Cash	5%

Simple Moderate Portfolio

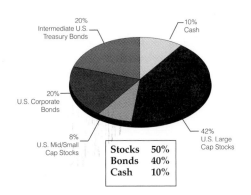

20%
Intermediate U.S.
Treasury Bonds

10%
Cash

20%
U.S. Corporate
Bonds

8%
U.S. Mid/Small
Cap Stocks

42%
U.S. Large
Cap Stocks

Stocks	50%
Bonds	40%
Cash	10%

Simple All Equity Portfolio

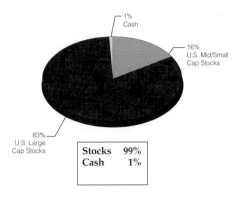

1%
Cash

16%
U.S. Mid/Small
Cap Stocks

83%
U.S. Large
Cap Stocks

Stocks	99%
Cash	1%

CHART 10-1

Investing a Million Before the Crash

Assume you inherit $1,000,000 in August 1929. The feel-good era of the Roaring '20s is still going strong. The U.S. has blossomed in the post-war years, and there is a general sense of pride in American industry - its strength and potential. Stock market investors in the U.S. are euphoric after years of sensational returns. The stocks leading the market are not speculative, they are industry leaders: Radio Corp. (RCA), General Electric, American Telephone, General Motors and United States Steel. These companies seemed irrevocably poised to continue to deliver on America's bright promise.

Without hesitation, you invest your new wealth following the criteria of one of the Simple Model Portfolios. Unknowingly, you have just invested 100% of your portfolio at the very top of a major bull market! Disaster strikes with the stock market crash of October 1929, followed by the worst bear market of the 20th century. A horrifying and debilitating period of relentlessly declining stock prices unfolds (see Chart 10-2).

Fortunately, you have a comprehensive understanding of the risks and rewards of your model portfolio. You stay the course and *rebalance* your stock, bond and cash allocations at the end of each calendar year to bring them back into alignment with your portfolio's asset allocation weightings. It certainly is not easy; the gloom and doomers are out in force (as usual), and the voice of calm reason is scoffed at and even ridiculed. Yet you stick to your guns....How bad is it? What happens to your $1,000,000? Did you blow your inheritance?

A Complete Market Cycle

The proper way to measure your results is over a full market cycle. Far too many market evaluations are hopelessly biased by either their starting date or ending date or both. The history of the U.S. stock market is one of sustained overall upward progress in market prices, which unfolds in periods of general advancement (bull markets), punctuated by sharp setbacks (bear markets).

The only fair evaluation of the stock market over spans of less than 15 to 20 years is to both begin and end at the exact same point in the market cycle - from one bull market peak to the next or one bear market through to the following one.

As you entered the markets at the very peak in stock prices (September 1, 1929), the fair evaluation of your results would include the entire bear market (through June 1932) and the complete bull market that follows (through February 1937) - one full market cycle.

Chart 10-2 tracks the performance of each asset class as well as inflation/deflation from the bull market peak in September, 1929, through the following bull market peak in February, 1937.

The Great Depression Market Cycle
(August 1929 through February 1937)
Annual Returns from Stocks, Bonds, Cash and Inflation*

Year	Inflation/ <Deflation>	U.S. Treasury Bills	U.S. 5-Year Treasury Bonds	Long-term Corporate Bonds	Large Cap Stocks	Mid/ Small Cap Stocks
1929**	-0.9%	1.6%	3.8%	3.4%	-31.2%	-33.9%
1930	-6.0	2.4	6.7	4.7	-24.9	-35.2
1931	-9.5	1.1	-2.3	-5.3	-43.3	-46.5
1932	-10.3	1.0	8.8	16.8	-8.2	-6.0
1933	0.5	0.3	1.8	-0.1	54.0	107.0
1934	2.0	0.2	9.0	10.0	-1.4	12.3
1935	3.0	0.2	7.0	5.0	47.7	43.8
1936	1.2	0.2	3.1	7.5	33.9	38.6
1937***	1.0	0.0	-0.2	1.2	5.9	8.2

Sources: © *Computed using data from* Stocks, Bonds, Bills & Inflation 2012 Yearbook™ *Ibbotson Associates, Chicago; Center for Research in Security Prices (CRSP) University of Chicago*

*   Total returns include interest, dividends and capital gains or losses.
**   September through December
*** January through February

CHART 10-2

Historical Note:
The bull market of the 1920s peaked in August 1929. The worst bear market of this century began in earnest with the infamous crash of October that same year. It was not straight down as there were substantial rallies to the upside along the way. The market finally bottomed in the summer of 1932. From that very low point, the stock market turned around and began one of its most rewarding bull markets. This bull market experienced several steep setbacks on its way to a peak in February 1937.

Chart 10-3 follows the progress of the four Simple Model Portfolios on a year-by-year basis from the very top of the Roaring '20s bull market, through the devastation of the Great Depression's bear market and on through the completion of the bull market that peaked in February 1937. This is one complete market cycle. Each simple model begins with $1,000,000 as of September 1, 1929. Returns are reflected on both a nominal basis (what shows up on your brokerage statement) and on a real return basis (the change in your wealth).

Simple Model Portfolios in the Great Depression
(September, 1929 through February, 1937)
$1,000,000 PORTFOLIO: CHANGE IN VALUE OVER THE MARKET CYCLE**

End of Year	Value of Sept. '29 U.S. $*	CONSERVATIVE (30-50-20) Nominal U.S. $	Real* U.S. $	MODERATE (50-40-10) Nominal U.S. $	Real* U.S. $	GROWTH (70-25-5) Nominal U.S. $	Real* U.S. $	ALL EQUITY (100-0-0) Nominal $	Real* U.S. $
1929†	1.01	926,000	935,000	858,000	867,000	788,000	797,000	687,000	696,000
1930	1.07	884,000	949,000	766,000	826,000	652,000	707,000	506,000	555,000
1931	1.17	754,000	900,000	587,000	712,000	444,000	549,000	287,000	367,000
1932	1.29	783,000	1,027,000	595,000	794,000	438,000	598,000	265,000	376,000
1933	1.29	936,000	1,222,000	783,000	1,041,000	629,000	856,000	428,000	607,000
1934	1.26	983,000	1,258,000	816,000	1,064,000	648,000	865,000	432,000	600,000
1935	1.22	1,152,000	1,438,000	1,027,000	1,308,000	870,000	1,135,000	633,000	862,000
1936	1.21	1,300,000	1,605,000	1,227,000	1,548,000	1,098,000	1,418,000	850,000	1,147,000
1937††	1.20	1,327,000	1,623,000	1,268,000	1,584,000	1,149,000	1,470,000	903,000	1,207,000
Avg. Annual Returns:		3.2%	5.5%	2.7%	5.2%	1.6%	4.4%	-1.1%	2.1%
For Comparison: 1972-2011			4.3%		5.0%		5.5%		5.9%

* Reflects <Deflation> / Inflation of Period
** Rebalanced Annually Utilizing Data from Chart 10-1
† September through December
†† January and February
Source: © Computed using data from Stocks, Bonds, Bills & Inflation 2012 Yearbook™ Ibbotson Associates, Chicago; Center for Research in Security Prices (CRSP) University of Chicago

CHART 10-3

Deflation's Effect

There is one factor that has an unusual bearing on this particular market cycle. The bear market of September 1929 through the end of 1932 is perhaps as noteworthy for its sustained *deflation* as for its falling stock prices.

Deflation is the opposite of inflation, i.e. the value or purchasing power of a dollar goes *up*, not down. Take a close look at Chart 10-2. The deflation from August 1929 to the end of 1932 added one-third to the purchasing power of every U.S. dollar. In isolation, this is a wonderful experience. Unfortunately, the accompanying economic conditions that bring about and sustain a period of deflation may not be pleasant at all. (Look at Japan's experience with deflation since the early 1990s to see that this is still true.)

Real returns, those adjusted for a change in the value of the currency unit, are much more important than nominal returns as far as measuring increases or decreases in wealth. It is the purchasing power of your portfolio you wish to increase. The same principle applies during this unusual period of deflation. The real return (buying power) is still more important than the nominal return. However, for deflation, returns are adjusted upward to reflect the increased purchasing power of the U.S. dollar.

Simple Moderate Portfolio: Step-By-Step

Assume your chosen portfolio was *50% domestic stocks* (42% large cap, and 8% mid/small cap), *40% bonds* (20% Intermediate Government Bonds and 20% Long-Term Corporates) and *10% cash* (30-day T-bills) - a Simple Domestic Moderate portfolio. Let's see how you navigated the full Great Depression cycle that unfolded after you invested your $1,000,000. The bottom-line results are shown in Chart 10-3 along with those of the other asset allocations. [To see how these results were actually developed, Chart A10-1 on page 250 in the Appendix provides a detailed presentation of the year-by-year gains and losses of each asset class, as well as the year-end rebalancing to maintain the desired asset allocations.]

Starting with $1,000,000 at the beginning of September 1929, your portfolio falls to $858,000 in just four months (a loss of 14% during the crash). In 1930, your portfolio falls to $766,000 - about 23% below where it was just 16 months before. The year 1931 is worse still; your rebalanced portfolio declines to $587,000 by year-end - down 41% from your original $1,000,000 in nominal terms. The vicious bear market reaches its low point at the end of May 1932. Your moderate portfolio is valued at $476,000, more than 52% below its beginning value.

Good news! (And you need it.) The value of the U.S. dollar has experienced a substantial bull market. The number on your year-end 1932 brokerage statement - $595,000 - will actually purchase in goods and services what $794,000 would have purchased in August 1929. Therefore, the real value of your portfolio has declined only a little over 20%.

The bull market for stocks, which began in the summer of 1932, now begins to significantly improve the numbers on your brokerage statement. By the end of 1933, your portfolio is up to $783,000, while your wealth (purchasing power) now exceeds that of your original inheritance.

The year 1934 sees further improvement, and 1935 is a truly banner year. Even your brokerage statement now shows your account to be above your initial investment. The year 1936 and the first two months of 1937 provide more big returns for your portfolio. By the end of February 1937, your brokerage statement reads $1,268,000…a 27% nominal gain from September 1929.

Taking into consideration the deflation/inflation for the entire 7½-year cycle, your wealth in August 1929 dollars stands at $1,584,000 - almost a 60% real gain - or 5.2% compounded annually! This is nearly identical to the 5.0% real annualized gain of the Moderate Balanced Portfolio during the modern era (1972 – 2011). (See Chapter 9) This outcome is probably much better than most people would believe possible for the market cycle that included the worst stock market conditions of this century.

Observations and Conclusions

Economic Tragedy

The Great Depression was the worst economic period of this century in the United States. The financial dislocations reached much further and deeper than the stock market alone. Joblessness reached 25 percent. The size of the American economy shrunk by *one-third*. Much of the confidence in the new American dream of perpetual prosperity was greatly eroded.

There is no one source to blame for a tragedy of such immense proportions. The relatively new Federal Reserve made serious mistakes, both in the boom period of the late 1920s and in the first few years of the Depression (shrinking the money supply by over 30%) and Congress thought it could dictate trade rules to the world (Smoot-Hawley Tariff).

The unsupervised stock market (the Securities and Exchange Commission and the National Association of Securities Dealers did not yet exist) encouraged highly speculative commodities-style stock trading. Stocks could be bought with as little as 10% of the purchase price paid in cash and 90% borrowed from the broker. (margin) Therefore, a minimal 10% decline in the value of a stock would force additional principal to be paid in (margin call) or the whole position would be lost. Thankfully, much has changed since that unfortunate period in U.S. history.

Stock Market Lessons

For long-term investors (as opposed to speculators or traders), the stock market's ebb and flow in this period should provide important lessons and confirmations.

> *Bull markets*, no matter how apparently sound the underpinnings, no matter how good the economic conditions, are followed by bear markets.

Bear markets, no matter how pernicious the economic conditions, no matter how deep the damage, are followed by bull markets.

There are no guarantees. Even a full market cycle does not guarantee that stocks will always be the best portfolio investment. It takes a period of 30 years for history to prove stocks are *always* the better investment over bonds and cash.

Do not buy stocks on margin. Buying stocks using leverage leaves you vulnerable to complete loss during periods of major market declines. It robs you of your ability to stay the course with your plan.

Stocks were truly devastated by the bear market of 1929-1932. Even the following bull market (1932-1937) did not quite restore the full loss in nominal dollars. Fortunately, this was a one-of-a-kind event since 1900.

Conclusion

The conventional wisdom is that the Great Depression virtually wiped out all investors and that there was no clear path to avoid the destruction in paper assets. This leaves many investors with a deep-seated, gripping fear of a repeat of 1929. The facts from the full period paint a somewhat different picture.

In fact, the 3.2% and 2.7% nominal returns from the Conservative and Moderate Simple Models were substantially better than the 0.9% average annual riskless return from T-bills. Even the Growth Portfolio's 1.6% average annual return was substantially better than that of cash. Balanced portfolios more than held their own - even in the market cycle containing the worst bear market of the modern financial era.

 This performance from balanced portfolios is one of the least known attributes of investment history. Balanced portfolios have wonderful risk-squelching characteristics that can serve the long-term investor and provide both comfort and confidence in uncertain times.

11

The Right Portfolio
For You

Introduction

The Model Portfolios introduced in Chapter 9 provide a wide cross-section of risks and rewards. One of those models is likely a sound choice to serve as the fundamental structure of your Wealth and Retirement Portfolio. You may already know which one is right for you. If you are uncertain as to a choice, there are three very important factors to consider: your personal financial situation, your likely reaction to market setbacks of varying intensity and the specific time horizon over which your investment portfolio will be held.

In uncertain investment environments, it is more important than ever to understand both your portfolio's risk/reward characteristics and your own risk tolerance.

"Know thyself"

— Socrates

Before You Select a Model Portfolio

As stated in this book's introduction, this is not a book about financial planning, as important as that area is. Therefore, you need to undertake the following, either by yourself or with the help of a financial planning expert.

- *Analyze your financial situation.* Put your Wealth and Retirement Portfolio on paper (or on computer).

- *Determine your major financial objectives.* Partial or full retirement? Early or later retirement? The idea is to estimate how many years of growth and new investment you anticipate versus the number of years you will be taking an income from your Wealth and Retirement Portfolio.

- *Prepare a retirement budget.* A realistic projection of your expenses in today's dollars that provides for your basic needs and a separate calculation of the non-essentials that will make your retirement enjoyable.

Charts A1-1 through A1-6 in the Appendix (pages 240-245) will help you evaluate the other side of your ledger - the maximum sustainable income you can plan on during retirement from your current portfolio and your future contributions into 401(k)-type programs. These charts illustrate varying average annual returns on your investments and illustrate the retirement income that is possible from a full range of long-term rates of return. (Chapter 12 will evaluate in detail the maximum sustainable retirement income from each of the domestic model portfolios under a full range of inflation and market conditions.)

The critical decision as to which Model Portfolio may be most appropriate for your Wealth and Retirement Portfolio is also influenced by the following:

- *Diversification.* The Model Portfolios set forth in Chapter 9 assume broad diversification within each stock asset class. However, your particular portfolio may not make this possible. For example, you may have a substantial commitment to your company's stock. A single stock has an undiversifiable risk that results from factors unique to a particular company. You may want to reduce risks in the balance of your portfolio to offset any such unavoidable and unique risks.

- *Income.* Once your Wealth and Retirement Portfolio begins to distribute income for your retirement, a greater prudence may well be necessary (a lower volatility asset allocation).

  As will be discussed thoroughly in Chapter 12, the percentage of income you can comfortably take from your retirement portfolio is subject to several assumptions including market conditions.

Simple "Formulas" That Don't Work

Regrettably, there is no black box you can plug some numbers into that will spit out the right portfolio for you. One-size-fits-all formulas should be ignored.

For instance, one such formula in the popular media is to establish a portfolio in which the percentage allocated to bonds is equal to your current age, with the balance to be put in stocks. This implies that it is appropriate for every 40-year-old to hold 40% in bonds. And, likewise, that every 60-year-old should allocate 60% to bonds.

Such a naïve formula would result in substantial and needless opportunity loss in wealth building or retirement income for most of its followers.

For those 40-year-olds and even 60-year-olds who understand and accept market fluctuations, both emotionally and intellectually, the higher long-term returns from portfolios with a larger commitment to equities may be more appropriate choices for many years to come in their lives.

After all, 40-year-olds should be building retirement portfolios planned to last for 50 years! This combines their remaining wealth building years (before retirement) and income distribution years (after retirement). And those who are 60 years of age should plan for a time horizon of at least 30 years for their retirement portfolios.

The Voice of Experience

And what about Phil Carret? This legendary investor died at age 101 in 1997. He was truly the most experienced investment manager in America. He started the Pioneer Mutual Fund in 1928 and managed client funds right up to the day he died - from the 1929 crash through the 1987 crash and every bull and bear market in between.

In his 55-year tenure as manager of the Pioneer Fund, a $10,000 investment in the fund would have grown to $28.3 million. By contrast, the same investment in the Dow Jones Industrial Average would have grown to only $3.8 million. (This record inspired market wizard Warren Buffett to praise Carret as having "the best long-term investment record of anyone in America.") Should Carret have avoided stocks altogether because of his age? Let's see what he had to say at age 98 on "Wall $treet Week with Louis Rukeyser," April 28, 1995.

RUKEYSER: "What would be your (investment policy) advice to some kid of, say, 65?"

CARRET: "Buy 30% bonds and 70% common stocks." (Basically, the Balanced Growth Model Portfolio)

RUKEYSER: "And that would be the same (advice for someone of age) 75 and 85?

CARRET: "Same thing."

This was a winning investment policy for Carret *because* of his personal comfort with its risks and rewards. Even at age 100, he was not tempted to change what worked for him. This is the level of commitment to which every long-term investor should aspire.

Where is Your Threshold for Pain?

A basic premise of this book is that the more prepared you are for the inevitable setbacks that are cooked-in-the-mix of your asset allocation, the less likely you will be foiled by the great enemy of long-term investment success - fear.

> "Fear leads to panic, panic breeds the inability to distinguish between temporary declines and permanent losses. That, in turn, leads to the well-documented propensity of investors to be massive sellers of good investments near market bottoms.
>
> "Success is purely a function of two things: (1) recognition of the inevitability of major market declines; and (2) emotional/behavioral preparation to regard such declines as...non-events..."
>
> —Nick Murray, *Investment Advisor* magazine, April, 1996

Not every investor has the same threshold for pain. To some investors, a 15% decline in their Wealth and Retirement Portfolio is extremely painful - prepared or not. Others, once prepared, can treat 30% declines as basically non-events.

Where do you fit? Numbers on a page have a way of appealing to your left brain, your intelligence. If they appeal to your emotions at all, it is usually to the other emotion that drives investment decisions - greed.

Right (Brain) Choice

Right now, you need to fully activate your right brain, your feelings. Call up any of your investment fears.

Select the model portfolio that you think most closely matches your financial facts and objectives or is simply your intuitive choice. Open this book to that portfolio's Historical Risk/Reward chart in Chapter 9. Look at the setbacks that this portfolio has incurred on its way to delivering its long-term return. Your Wealth and Retirement Portfolio will more than likely last that many years - and randomly incur setbacks of that same magnitude.

How will you feel when these losses unfold over periods of 18 months or more in your Wealth and Retirement Portfolio? Stomach-turning reactions are normal. As Richard Thaler, the economist at the University of Chicago, has pointed out, "Losing $100 hurts about twice as much as winning $100 gives you pleasure." Could this feeling induce fear or panic that will cause you to take actions that are inappropriate for your long-term success?

> "Successful investment management depends to a large extent on the emotional stability of the individual, particularly during periods of strain and stress, and on his ability to overcome the severe psychological hurdles present during crucial periods." —Ragnar D. Naess, *Readings in Financial Analysis and Investment Management*, 1963

Many financial plans are foiled by poor emotional planning. Don't let your plan be overturned during the stressful market periods such as those in our current period of uncertainty. If you are seeking to maximize the predictability of your long-term performance, select an appropriate asset allocation. Any one of the Model Portfolios is an excellent choice depending on the rewards you want and the risks you are willing to live with through all its inherent ups and downs.

Time Horizon

It has been stressed that the principles of this book only apply to long-term portfolios, i.e. portfolios expected to see you throughout your retirement and perhaps to be left to your heirs. Not knowing how long your needs for retirement income will last, plan on your portfolio providing an inflation adjusted income well beyond the life expectancy of you and your spouse. Therefore, if you or your spouse are under 65 years of age, your Wealth and Retirement Portfolio is definitely long-term.

If you are older than 65 or are planning for a portfolio that will last less than 20 years, you should take into consideration the full *range* of possible returns from your selected asset allocation policy for the time period you have allocated.

 Each model portfolio's long-term reward (as shown in Chapter 9) is the historic average toward which it has gravitated over the very long run. However, the shorter the time period being evaluated, the higher the variance in average annual returns. Charts 11-1 through 11-4 illustrate the range of average annual returns from the Model Portfolios for all 5-year, 10-year, 15-year and 20-year periods within the 1972-2011 period. Commentary and investment suggestions follow each chart. Pay close attention to the range of returns that each model portfolio has provided over your investment time horizon. Your planning should take all of the possible outcomes into consideration.

How Long is Your Investment Horizon?

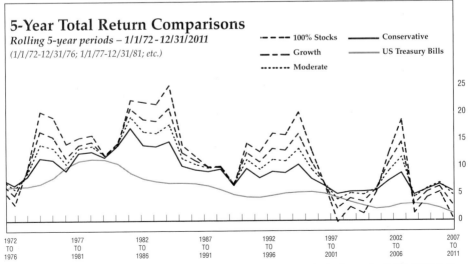

Each point on this graph represents the end of a 5-year investment period. The first point (1972-1976) is the 5-year total return (annualized) for each portfolio beginning 1/1/72.

CHART 11-1

- *5-Year Investment Horizon*. Each model portfolio has provided a wide range of 5-year returns. The Conservative portfolio has provided average annual (nominal) returns from as low as 4.8% to as high as 16.8% for the 36 5-year periods beginning with 1972. The range of annualized returns for 5-year periods from the other Model Portfolios are as follows: 3.8% to 18.7% for the Moderate portfolio, 2.3% to 20.3% for the Growth portfolio and -0.3% to 24.3% for the All Equity model portfolio. As you can see, there is not much that is predictable in such a short investment period.

Another way of looking at a 5-year horizon may be summed up by the question, "How often and by how much did each domestic model portfolio underperform the riskless return of cash equivalents (30-day U.S. Treasury bills)?" (The return from Treasury bills is included on each of these four charts.) The Conservative Model underperformed U.S. Treasury bills in only one of the 36 5-year periods. The Moderate Portfolio underperformed Treasury bills in three periods, the Growth Portfolio three periods also and the All Equity Portfolio in in six of the 36 periods.

For *any* 5-year period in the Inflation Era, the maximum annualized percentage return *under* that of U.S. Treasury bills for the Conservative Balanced portfolio was less than 1% annualized. By contrast, the Growth Balanced portfolio has underperformed U.S. Treasury bills by as much as 1.4% per year in a 5-year period, while the 100% Stocks portfolio underperformed cash by as much as 4.4% per year in one 5-year period.

 With a 5-year time horizon, either the Conservative Balanced or Moderate Balanced portfolio would be the best choice. They provided both a low *risk* of underperforming cash (one or three periods out of 36) and a low *degree* of underperformance during such periods. Yet, on average, the Conservative model has outperformed Treasury bills by an average of 3.3%, annualized over all 5-year periods and the Moderate Balanced Portfolio outperformed by 4.0% annualized.

Each of the other Model Portfolios should be approached much more cautiously for such a short investment horizon as five years. Although the risk of underperformance may be low, the degree of underperformance is more substantial and may jeopardize the achievement of the goal for which the money is invested.

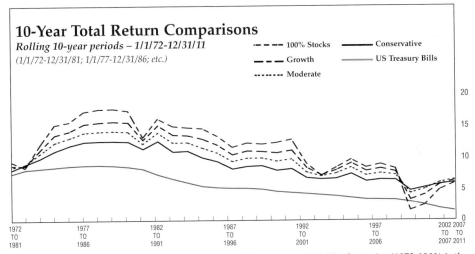

10-Year Total Return Comparisons
Rolling 10-year periods – 1/1/72-12/31/11
(1/1/72-12/31/81; 1/1/77-12/31/86; etc.)

- - - 100% Stocks   ——— Conservative
- - - Growth   ~~~~ US Treasury Bills
······· Moderate

Each point on this graph represents the end of a 10-year investment period. The first point (1972-1981) is the 10-year total return (annualized) for each portfolio beginning 1/1/72.

CHART 11-2

- *10-Year Investment Horizon.* Each model portfolio continues to deliver a large range of average returns in the 31 10-year periods reflected in Chart 11-2. The Conservative portfolio ranges from a low 10-year return of 5.1% to a high of 13.0%, not that much different from its range of 5-year returns particularly on the low end of the range. The Moderate portfolio's 10-year average annual returns range from a low of 5.2% to a high of 14.6%. The Growth Balanced portfolio ranges from 3.6% to 16.2%, and All Equity has a range of 1.9% to 18.2%. The most noticeable *improvement* at a 10-year time horizon over that of a 5-year horizon is the progressively better low-end of the range of returns as one moves from Conservative to All Equity.

As for the degree of underperforming cash, neither the Conservative, Moderate nor Growth portfolios ever underperform Treasury bills in the 31 10-year periods. The All Equity model portfolio underperformed cash in two 10-year periods, the worst being a full 1.3% average annual underperformance.

 Therefore, with a 10-year time horizon, it appears that the Conservative, Moderate and Growth portfolios are all quite acceptable. On the other hand, the All Equity portfolio in a 10-year time horizon carries some risk of underperforming Treasury bills but probably not by a margin great enough to jeopardize the goals set for the portfolio.

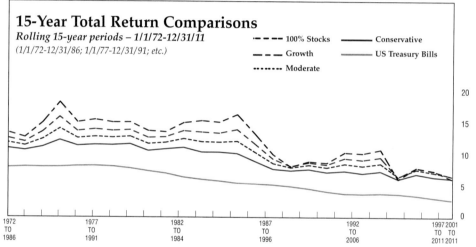

15-Year Total Return Comparisons

Rolling 15-year periods – 1/1/72-12/31/11
(1/1/72-12/31/86; 1/1/77-12/31/91; etc.)

- - - - 100% Stocks   ——— Conservative
- - - Growth   ——— US Treasury Bills
······· Moderate

Each point on this graph represents the end of a 15-year investment period. The first point (1972-1986) is the 15-year total return (annualized) for each portfolio beginning 1/1/72.

CHART 11-3

- *15-Year Time Horizon.* The graph of 15-year returns (Chart 11-3) begins to smooth out considerably compared to the five-year and 10-year charts. Yet there is still a considerable range of returns. The Conservative portfolio produces average annual returns of between 6.3% at the low end and 12.4% at the high end. The range for the Moderate portfolio is between 6.6% and 13.0%. For the Growth portfolio it is between 6.6% and 16.1%, and for All Equity the range is from 6.2% to 18.4%.

Fifteen years turns out to be a significant time horizon in two respects. All four Model Portfolios outperform U.S. Treasury bills in each of the 26 15-year periods. In addition, at 15 years, the Growth portfolio always outperformed the Moderate portfolio, which in turn always outperformed the Conservative portfolio. However, the same cannot be said of the All Equity portfolio whose 15-year rate of return dipped below that of the Growth portfolio in five periods – but never by more than 0.5% per year.

Whereas any of the four domestic models are acceptable with a 15-year investment horizon, the Growth portfolio appears to be a better choice than All Equity.

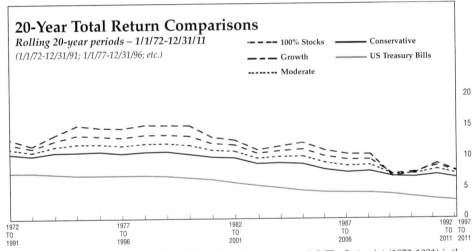

20-Year Total Return Comparisons
Rolling 20-year periods – 1/1/72-12/31/11
(1/1/72-12/31/91; 1/1/77-12/31/96; etc.)

- – – – – 100% Stocks   ———— Conservative
- — – — Growth   ———— US Treasury Bills
- ······· Moderate

Each point on this graph represents the end of a 20-year investment period. The first point (1972-1991) is the 20-year total return (annualized) for each portfolio beginning 1/1/72.

CHART 11-4

- _20-Year Time Horizon._ Contrasting Chart 11-4 with the other three charts demonstrates why this book has chosen a 20-year time horizon or greater as the appropriate time horizon for long-term portfolios. By 20 years, the returns from the various Model Portfolios have flattened out considerably.

 When planning for time periods of 20 years or less, perhaps a variation in an old saying is appropriate, "Plan for the worst, expect the average." In other words, you may want to prepare two estimated return calculations, one utilizing the long-term average annual rate of return from Chapter 9 and one utilizing the worst-case scenario as indicated by the bottom portion of the range depicted on these charts. If your time horizon is longer than 20 years, then the *average* annual return shown for each model portfolio in Chapter 9 is most likely your best planning choice.

Real Returns

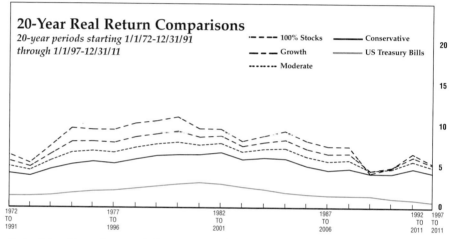

Each point on this graph represents the average annualized real return for a particular 20-year period. Real returns measure wealth accumulation by removing the inflation component from nominal rates of return.

Viewed from the perspective of 20-year real returns, the Conservative Balanced and Moderate Balanced asset allocation policies have been relatively stable, whereas Growth Balanced and particularly 100% Stocks have provided a wide variation in real returns.

CHART 11-5

Charts 11-1 through 11-4 reflect "nominal returns," those not adjusted for inflation/deflation. Even though this is the way we usually think about rates of return, it is not the only way - particularly when planning long-term.

Chart 11-5 reflects the annualized *real* returns over 20-year time periods beginning with 1972-1991 and ending with 1992-2011. This chart covers both a predominantly inflationary period (1972-1981) and a predominantly disinflationary period (2000-2011). The returns reflected in this chart are those above or below the actual inflation of that particular 20-year period.

A big part of the price tag for higher returns has been increased *volatility*. As this study demonstrates, volatility is not the same as being *at risk* of not achieving your retirement goals. Over the past four decades, a more aggressive asset allocation nearly always outperformed a more conservative one when viewed from time periods of 20 years or longer.

Conclusion

There are many factors that could impact the selection of the optimal Model Portfolio for any investor. These include: financial objectives, retirement living needs and emotional sensitivity of portfolio declines.

In other words, part of the decision may include objective factors and partly it may be for subjective reasons. In the uncertain market conditions that have persisted since the year 2000, it's likely that most investors have experienced greater anxiety about their investments than in the 1990s or 1980s. Thus careful examination of the declines and recoveries of each Model Portfolio - as displayed on their Historical Risk/Reward Charts in Chapter 9 - will be a very important consideration in making a final selection.

12

Maximizing Your Retirement Income

Introduction

How much income can your portfolio reasonably provide throughout your retirement? This is a critically important question to answer *before* you begin withdrawing an income. Certain choices will have a dramatic affect on the answer. Do you wish to leave a legacy to your heirs? Do you want to fully or partially increase your income to reflect changes in the cost of living?

You should also take into consideration factors over which you have no control but still may significantly influence the amount that your portfolio can distribute during your full retirement. One such factor is the unfolding of worst-case market conditions early in your retirement. In an uncertain investment environment, this is an important consideration. This chapter will explore the impact of each of these choices and factors on the four Model Portfolios from Chapter 9.

"Nine-tenths of wisdom is being wise in time."

— Theodore Roosevelt

No Room for Error

Many retirees face the financial side of their retirement with an understandable touch of fear. Before retiring, employment income paid the bills. Investments were for the future, and there was time to make up for any mistakes. Suddenly, it's very different.

One of the biggest challenges for those contemplating retirement is to determine how much they can comfortably take out of their portfolio each year without prematurely depleting it. While there is no precise answer, a realistic, time tested calculation is far better than no estimate at all.

Four Considerations in Calculating Retirement Income

There are four major considerations in determining the maximum withdrawal rate from your retirement portfolio.

- Your portfolio's expected long-term rate of return;

- The appropriate adjustment for inflation;

- Your intention with regard to maintaining or depleting the principal of your retirement portfolio; and

- Your life expectancy (or how long your portfolio will provide an income).

Notice that your level of spending is *not* considered here. Although your retirement spending level is a critical, separate variable, it really does not influence what a portfolio *can* pay out over its full term.

Assumptions for Each Model Portfolio

In order to calculate the maximum withdrawal percentage that each model portfolio (introduced in Chapter 9) could pay out annually during retirement, the following assumptions are made.

Historical Performance. The actual performance of the Model Portfolios and the Consumer Price Index (CPI) in the 1972-2011 period is used as the platform for this study.

Life Expectancy. Each model portfolio is assumed to provide income for 40 years. (This is well beyond the average number of years retirees take income out of his/her/their portfolio.)

Principal: Maintain or Deplete. There are two types of illustrations for each model portfolio. A *Perpetual Portfolio* in which principal is maintained (adjusted for inflation) and a *Spend-it-All Portfolio* (Spending My Children's Inheritance) in which principal is used to enhance income over 40 years before being depleted.

Initial Withdrawal Rate. The maximum withdrawal rate for the *first* year of retirement is shown as a percentage of the Wealth and Retirement Portfolio just prior to retirement. The purchasing power of this initial distribution is held up throughout retirement by adjusting the original year's income by an appropriate measure of inflation.

Chart 12-1 shows the maximum percentage that each model portfolio could pay out in the first year of retirement and still satisfy all of the assumptions above. (Charts A12-1 through A12-4 in the Appendix illustrate the year-by-year calculations and results for the Moderate Model Portfolio that are summarized within this chapter.) Real returns for any long period of time are likely to approximate those of the 1972-2011 period, therefore these initial withdrawal rates are appropriate for your own future planning.

Maximum Retirement Income – Full CPI Adjustment

Retirement income, once set by this percentage, adjusts annually by the full change in CPI.

Model Portfolios	Spend-it-All Portfolio (40 Years' Income)	Perpetual Portfolio (Perpetual Income)
Conservative Model	4.7%	3.8%
Moderate Model	5.1%	4.4%
Growth Model	5.5%	4.8%
All Equity (100% Stocks) Model	5.7%	5.2%

CHART 12-1

Example: A new retiree that has selected the Moderate Model Portfolio for her $1,000,000 Wealth and Retirement Portfolio. According to Chart 12-1, she could withdraw up to $51,000 for income in her first year of retirement ($1,000,000 x 5.1%) and adjust this $51,000 upward by the full change in the CPI index each year for 40 years before her principal is depleted. Or, she could take out $44,000 in her first year of retirement ($1,000,000 x 4.4%) and adjust this amount upward by the full change in the CPI index in perpetuity. Under this last scenario, the full inflation-adjusted value of the $1,000,000 portfolio should be more or less maintained over time.

Your Inflation Rate

Suppose you want a higher first year withdrawal rate than that shown in Chart 12-1 for a particular model portfolio. One obvious choice would be to adopt a more aggressive model for your Wealth and Retirement Portfolio.

Another change of assumptions that may be appropriate is in the inflation adjustment. It is quite possible that the pay-out from your Wealth and Retirement Portfolio will not require an automatic raise by the full percentage increase in the CPI each year. Some of your expenses may be fixed, some may be stable, some may decline as your retirement unfolds. Obviously, you will gauge your actual expenses and raise your income accordingly. Perhaps your own personal inflation rate may only be two-thirds of the general rate *as registered by the CPI statistic.* This is more consistent with spending patterns of retirees as reported in a study by the U.S. Department of Labor (DOL).

In addition, the CPI itself has come under criticism by noted economists; and even Alan Greenspan, the former Chairman of the Federal Reserve, stated in testimony to congress, "The (CPI) statistic is but an imprecise statistical proxy for inflation." He is also on record as stating that the reported CPI may overstate inflation by a full percentage point - about one-third of the projected 3.1% inflation rate. Therefore, estimating your personal inflation rate at two-thirds of the CPI rate may better recognize the U.S. economy's true rate of inflation and particularly your own.

Therefore, a second set of maximum first year withdrawal rates have been calculated assuming your retirement income need only increase at 67% of reported CPI. These numbers are reflected in Chart 12-2. *Of course, this lower than inflation pay-out would not apply to Perpetual Portfolios which would see real inflation-adjusted payouts decline to very low levels 40+ years in the future.*

Maximum Retirement Income – Two-Thirds Inflation (CPI) Adjustment

Retirement income, once set by this percentage, adjusts annually by two-thirds of the change in CPI.

Model Portfolios	Spend-it-All Portfolio (40 Years' Income)
Conservative Model	6.1%
Moderate Model	6.5%
Growth Model	6.9%
All Equity (100% Stocks) Model	7.1%

CHART 12-2

This particular change in the inflation adjustment allows for a substantial increase in the initial withdrawal rate from your portfolio at retirement. From our prior example, the new retiree with a portfolio of $1,000,000 can add $14,000 to her beginning annual income at retirement (from $51,000 to $65,000) if she adjusts this higher initial income by only two-thirds of the CPI index over time. However, the real buying power of the income in future years will decline and eventually be lower than that illustrated in Chart 12-1.

Worst-Case Market Conditions

One other consideration should be addressed. As pointed out, the calculations in this chapter follow the thesis presented in Chapter 6 that the year 1972 is perhaps the best representative year for beginning a long-term market analysis, because it allows for the inclusion of all major asset classes (rigorous data is available).

However, a search of the available data back to 1926 reveals that 1968 was the very worst year to begin retirement. Not only was the stock market beginning one of its worst six-year periods ever, but inflation was just starting a long, dramatic rise. The impact of retiring at just the wrong time is calculated for each model portfolio in Chart 12-3. Like Chart 12-2, this chart assumes retirement income is adjusted by two-thirds of the annual change in CPI.

Maximum Retirement Income – Worst-Case Initial Market Conditions

Retirement income, beginning in the worst conditions of the Inflation Era, adjusts annually by two-thirds of the change in CPI.

Model Portfolios	Spend-it-All Portfolio (40 Years' Income)
Conservative Model	5.5%
Moderate Model	5.7%
Growth Model	5.9%
All Equity (100% Stocks) Model	5.8%

CHART 12-3

Comparing Chart 12-3 with Chart 12-2 demonstrates the impact of *initial* market conditions on the amount of income a portfolio can afford to pay-out.

Notice the unevenness of the effect on the four Model Portfolios. As with Chapter 10's discussion of portfolios in the Great Depression, the less growth-oriented the model portfolio (percentage of stocks), the less damage inflicted by worst-case market conditions. For example, the Conservative model's maximum pay-out was only reduced by six-tenths of one percent (from 6.1% down to 5.5%), while the 100% Stocks model suffered a 1.3% percent reduction (from 7.1% down to 5.8%).

Conclusion: Considering the Choices

Your choices as to how aggressively your retirement portfolio is invested, what kind of inflation adjustment to apply and whether to maintain your portfolio as a legacy for future generations will all impact on how much retirement income you can take from your Wealth and Retirement Portfolio.

Model Portfolio Choice. These charts provide valuable additional input in choosing a model portfolio to emulate during retirement. Under normal market conditions, looking from one model portfolio to the next (as measured by a higher percentage dedicated to stocks) adds between 10% to 20% to your sustainable retirement income.

Inflation Adjustment. Planning for a retirement income that fully adjusts for annual changes in CPI has a big price tag. It may be worth it, but perhaps it isn't. In the 1972-2011 period and likely in any future period, adjusting your retirement income by 67% of the annual change in CPI (instead of 100%) allows for between 20% and 30% higher *initial* retirement income.

Perpetual or Spend-it-All. This decision has a substantial effect on your retirement income. For those who wish to leave an estate behind approximately equal to the real value of their portfolio at retirement, the reduction in the maximum retirement income that could be paid out in the 1972-2011 period was between 19% (from 4.7% to 3.8% in a Conservative Model Portfolio) and 10% (from 5.7% to 5.2% in a 100% Stocks portfolio) with full inflation adjustment. This is also a likely consequence going forward.

Market Conditions. Market conditions are a more troubling topic. Certainly those who retired in 1968 did not know at the time that they were looking down a double-barreled shotgun of much higher inflation and extremely poor market performance for the immediately following years. Those 1968 retirees, who were anticipating a continuance of market conditions that existed just prior to 1968, would face some unhappy choices if they paid out the maximum retirement income allowed by more normal market conditions. They would run out of retirement income well short of the 40 years anticipated.

The impact of poor market conditions diminishes the further in the future they unfold. The best advice is *be prepared*. Know your worst-case scenario and be prepared to live within it. If extremely poor market conditions do unfold early in your retirement, you will be glad you were ready.

Section IV

*Creating and Managing
Your Wealth and Retirement
Portfolio*

Overview
of Section IV

Whereas your asset allocation policy provides the structure for your portfolio, you still need to choose a comprehensive strategy to implement and maintain it.

We present both sides of a popular debate within the investment community. Is it better to invest in low cost, passively managed index funds or pursue superior actively managed mutual funds?

This section creates passively managed portfolios of index funds and exchange-traded funds (ETFs) that match the Model Portfolios of Chapter 9. Even for those investors who prefer to invest in actively managed mutual funds, a "dummy" indexed portfolio should serve as a benchmark to measure their actual portfolio's performance.

We then reinforce one of the most critical rules of successful investing, *staying the course*. It applies equally to investing with index funds or actively managed funds.

This section also demonstrates how inflation and taxes affect an investor's portfolio and provides strategies for minimizing taxes.

Understandably, many investors do not have the time, interest or inclination to take on the all-important task of ongoing portfolio management. Our book concludes with a thorough analysis for selecting an investment adviser. It also describes the best way to avoid a "Madoff" style "Ponzi scheme". This could be the "one decision" to fulfill the strategies outlined in this book.

After reading section IV, you will be able to decide what implementation strategy is the right fit for you.

13

The Great Debate: Active versus Passive Investing

Introduction

Over the last decade index fund investing, also known as passive investing, has become increasingly popular among investors. Index funds have many excellent qualities including low costs and tax efficiency.

Actively managed mutual funds offer a different set of strategic advantages such as reduced volatility or other special criteria. Yet, on average, actively managed mutual funds have slightly underperformed the major indexes because of their somewhat higher costs.

> *"How can institutional investors hope to outperform the market when, in effect, they are the market?"*

> \-   Charles D. Ellis,
> Former Chairman of the
> investment committee at Yale

Index Investing

Investing in index mutual funds and index ETFs (Exchange Traded Funds) is the simplest and most certain way to put your asset allocation policy in action. It virtually guarantees that you will achieve results that closely parallel those of your chosen Model Portfolio's asset allocation.

An index fund is structured to reproduce the return of a specific index or asset class. For instance, an S&P 500 index fund should closely mimic the performance of the S&P 500 index. To accomplish this, an index fund will normally buy the same stocks or bonds in the same proportions as the underlying index.

As index funds and ETFs are passively managed, they do not require the breadth and depth of personnel that actively managed funds employ for research and analysis. This allows for lower fund management fees. Trading costs within these funds are kept to a minimum so brokerage costs are also fairly low. The total cost differential between an index fund and an actively managed fund can easily run between 0.5% and 1.0% of fund assets per year. This is a head start with which index funds begin each year.

Offsetting this cost advantage is the somewhat higher volatility that index funds incur relative to the average managed fund. This is primarily due to index funds being fully invested through all market declines.

Some studies have attributed tax savings to index funds in taxable accounts. This is due to their low turnover of securities creating little in the way of capital gains. However, several studies, including one conducted by the No-Load Fund Analyst, have raised clouds over this issue. Many actively managed funds that have produced superior returns to index funds have actually distributed less in taxable gains and dividends, as they employ specific strategies to reduce taxable distributions.

Is an index fund strategy right for you? Your orientation toward investing is the main determinant. A general profile of a good candidate for an index fund strategy is shown below:

Index Funds and ETFs:

Issues to Consider	Candidate for Index Fund Strategy
Time for Investments	"I want to spend as little time on my investments as possible."
Interest Level in Investing	"Investments are boring."
Stress Level	"Uncertainties of investing are stressful."
Goals for Investment Performance	"Capturing market returns with normal ups and downs is okay with me."
Attitude Toward Fees	"I don't like paying any more in fees than I absolutely have to."
Temperament	"I have the fortitude to weather the full bear market declines."

Chart 13-1

If you choose this elegantly simple strategy of capturing average returns and average setbacks, you will never suffer below average performance! You will have completely harnessed the full long-term predictability of your asset allocation policy. In uncertain times, this provides a certain result.

Investing in Actively Managed Funds

Advocates of actively managed funds believe that experienced and successful investment managers can add value by either outperforming the index (that best represents their asset class) over time or reducing volatility during bear market declines. Active managers make judgments on economic, market, industry and/or company trends in their attempt to outperform. Even the best actively managed fund managers will not beat the indexes every year, but superior fund managers have achieved either higher returns, lower volatility or both over long periods of time.

You often hear that actively managed funds try to "beat the market". However, the real goal of investing with active managers should be to beat the INDEX of their particular benchmark, after all costs and fees are taken into account. A general profile of a good candidate to use actively managed mutual funds is shown below.

Managed Funds:

Issues to Consider	Candidate for Active Management Strategy
Time for Investments	"My schedule affords ample time for researching, evaluating and selecting actively managed funds."
Interest Level in Investing	"Investing is fun, interesting, challenging."
Stress Level	"Being totally at the mercy of the market (in index funds) is stressful."
Goals for Investment Performance	"I want to try to beat my benchmark AND/OR I want benchmark returns with less fluctuation in values."
Attitude Toward Fees	"Risk and returns are far more important than fees."
Temperament	"I would prefer to forgo some bull market gains in order to avoid full bear market declines."

CHART 13-2

Conclusion

Index funds and ETFs offer the certainty of matching market performance – for both good and bad. Actively managed funds offer the opportunity for above market returns and/or below market risk. Chapter 14 provides a detailed presentation of index funds and ETFs.

There are actively managed funds that have outperformed index funds representing their asset class over long periods of time – particularly on a risk adjusted basis (return per "unit" of risk). Chapter 15 presents a methodology for selecting superior actively managed mutual funds and provides several exemplary candidates.

Of course, there is nothing wrong with building a portfolio of mutual funds and ETFs that include both index and actively managed funds. In fact, this may be an excellent option which combines the best of both worlds.

14

Building a Portfolio or Benchmark using Index Funds or ETFs

Introduction

This chapter will turn the Model Portfolios developed in Chapter 9 into investable portfolios by identifying index funds and index ETFs to fill out those models. For those investors who want the certainty of an index approach, these portfolios are ready to go.

Those who choose to employ actively managed mutual funds should still monitor a "benchmark portfolio" of index funds or ETFs that best fits their asset allocation policy. *It is the best yardstick by which to measure performance.*

> *"Simplicity or singleness of approach is a greatly underestimated factor of market success."*
>
> - Garfield Drew (1941)
> (Well known investment adviser)

Index Fund/ETF Portfolios

As discussed in Chapter 13, there are index funds and index ETFs (Exchange Traded Funds) available for mimicking the performance of virtually any asset class – or slice of an asset class – that an investor would want.

In fact, there are so many choices today that even the process of finding and evaluating appropriate index funds/ETFs can be daunting.

In this chapter, we provide complete portfolios of both index funds and index ETFs that match the Model Portfolios which were developed in Chapter 9. For those investors who want the certainty of index investing for their Wealth and Retirement Portfolios, one of these portfolios should meet their needs.

For investors who wish to use actively managed mutual funds (or a mix of actively managed funds, index funds and individual securities), it is still important to assemble and monitor an index fund/ETF portfolio that matches their chosen asset allocation. The performance of the index fund/ETF portfolio will serve as a benchmark or yardstick for their actual portfolio's performance.

Today, there are numerous free providers of computer-modeling services for "dummy" portfolios. Most investment custodians provide them as do the Wall Street Journal and Barron's. Any of the portfolios developed in this chapter can be easily loaded into their software. This allows investors a convenient way to follow a benchmark of their chosen model portfolio.

Right and Wrong Yardsticks

Applying the wrong yardstick to portfolio performance is very common among individual investors.

By far the most common mis-measuring tool is the Dow Jones Industrial Average ("Dow"). When virtually anyone asks, "How did the market do today?" the normal response is the gain or loss in the Dow that day. In other words, the performance of just 30 very large stocks within the domestic stock market is the expected answer.

Unfortunately, this is very deceptive as the Dow includes no domestic mid-cap or small-cap stocks, no REITS and no international stocks.

And, this is just the beginning, for the very next question is, "How are you doing vs. 'the market'?" This pits your portfolio's performance against that of the Dow.

Using the Dow as your reference point would be appropriate only if your portfolio (or the stocks portion thereof) was made up of but one asset class - the giant Dow stocks. With any other asset allocation policy, such a comparison is apples to oranges. Using the wrong yardstick leads to the wrong conclusions about your portfolio's performance and soon may lead you to make inappropriate changes within your portfolio. After you have created your benchmark portfolio, you now have the perfect comparison.

Building a Benchmark Portfolio with Index Funds

The following four pie charts provide a portfolio of index mutual funds that matches the asset allocation of each of the Model Portfolios built in Chapter 9.

All Equity Allocation Using Index Funds

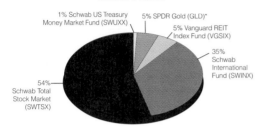

1% Schwab US Treasury Money Market Fund (SWUXX)
5% SPDR Gold (GLD)*
5% Vanguard REIT Index Fund (VGSIX)
35% Schwab International Fund (SWINX)
54% Schwab Total Stock Market (SWTSX)

Moderate Allocation Using Index Funds

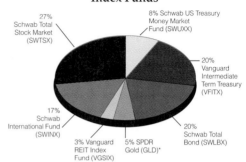

27% Schwab Total Stock Market (SWTSX)
8% Schwab US Treasury Money Market Fund (SWUXX)
20% Vanguard Intermediate Term Treasury (VFITX)
20% Schwab Total Bond (SWLBX)
5% SPDR Gold (GLD)*
3% Vanguard REIT Index Fund (VGSIX)
17% Schwab International Fund (SWINX)

Growth Allocation Using Index Funds

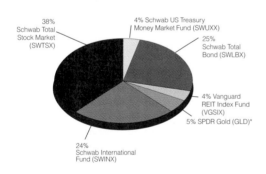

38% Schwab Total Stock Market (SWTSX)
4% Schwab US Treasury Money Market Fund (SWUXX)
25% Schwab Total Bond (SWLBX)
4% Vanguard REIT Index Fund (VGSIX)
5% SPDR Gold (GLD)*
24% Schwab International Fund (SWINX)

Conservative Allocation Using Index Funds

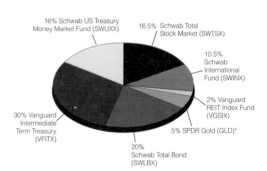

16% Schwab US Treasury Money Market Fund (SWUXX)
16.5% Schwab Total Stock Market (SWTSX)
10.5% Schwab International Fund (SWINX)
2% Vanguard REIT Index Fund (VGSIX)
5% SPDR Gold (GLD)*
20% Schwab Total Bond (SWLBX)
30% Vanguard Intermediate Term Treasury (VFITX)

For the Gold Allocation we recommend the SPDR Gold ETF instead of an index mutual fund (as of early 2012).

CHART 14-1

Exchange Traded Funds (ETF)

Exchange traded funds (ETFs) are like index funds but with the added flexibility of being traded throughout the trading day like a stock. Index funds and ETFs are both very low cost and are meant to track indexes for investors who do not want to pick stocks or utilize actively managed mutual funds.

The first ETFs mimicked major asset class indexes such as the S&P 500. Now investors can buy shares of ETFs that track the performance of small slices of the market, new customized indexes, or even leveraged bets on various indexes.

The Advantages of ETFs over Index Funds

As stated above, ETFs offer more trading flexibility. Unlike index mutual funds (and all other mutual funds), ETFs can be bought and sold throughout the trading day just like a stock. Index mutual funds, on the other hand, can only be bought or sold at the closing price at the end of trading each day. Some fund companies, such as Vanguard, even require that mutual fund trades be placed earlier in the day in order to buy or sell at the closing price.

ETFs can be sold short, leveraged on margin, or day traded just like stocks. They offer the certainty of index investing with the flexibility of stock trading. Investors have many more index choices with ETFs. Whereas index funds typically track large and liquid indexes, many ETFs are designed to follow market sectors (energy, technology, etc.), commodities, styles (growth, value) and much more.

ETFs are also more tax efficient than index funds. Jeremy Siegel explains this in the most recent (4th) edition of his book, *Stocks For The Long Run* (McGraw Hill, 2008). "ETFs are extremely tax efficient since, unlike mutual funds, they generate almost no capital gains either from the sales of other investors or from portfolio changes to the index. This is because swaps between the

ETFs and underlying shares are considered *exchanges in kind* and are not taxable events."

The Disadvantages of ETFs

Commissions

Because ETFs trade like a stock, an investor must pay a commission each time he buys or sells ETF shares. The commissions are generally small but even these commissions can eat into the returns of smaller accounts. (Mutual funds, on the other hand, can often be purchased without fees either directly from the mutual fund provider or on popular platforms like Charles Schwab's One Source Marketplace.)

Bid-Ask Spread

Just like stocks, ETFs trade on a bid-ask spread instead of at a closing NAV (Net Asset Value) as mutual funds do. The amount by which the ask price exceeds the bid price. (This is essentially the difference in price between the highest price that a buyer is willing to pay (currently) for an asset and the lowest price for which a seller is willing to sell it.) With ETFs that have large daily volumes this spread should not be significant. However investing in a less liquid ETF or investing in a small segment of the market may have a much larger bid-ask spread that can trim returns in a more meaningful way.

Tracking Error

When buying a share of either an index mutual fund or ETF, the expectation is to mimic the performance of the underlying index. Normally, index funds will generate returns extremely similar to the underlying index the fund is tracking. With ETFs, this is more hit or miss. Shares of the largest ETFs following the major indexes will track just as well as the index mutual funds.

HOWEVER, the smaller ETFs that are less liquid (or that invest in illiquid segments of the stock or bond markets) can have significant tracking error. Even some large ETFs have materially outperformed or underperformed their respective index over significant periods of time, particularly if there is either leverage or shorting within the ETF. These ETFs are designed to provide a multiple of an index's return by using leverage or provide the mirror image return of the index being followed by selling short the underlying securities.

Building a Benchmark Portfolio with ETFs

The following pie charts illustrate a portfolio of exchange traded funds that can be used to build a passive portfolio to track each asset allocation described in Chapter 9 or to measure the performance of your actively managed portfolio against – for both risks and rewards.

All Equity Allocation Using ETFs

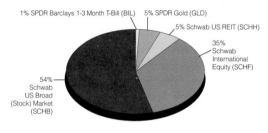

1% SPDR Barclays 1-3 Month T-Bill (BIL)   5% SPDR Gold (GLD)

5% Schwab US REIT (SCHH)

35% Schwab International Equity (SCHF)

54% Schwab US Broad (Stock) Market (SCHB)

Moderate Allocation Using ETFs

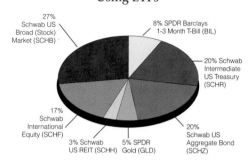

27% Schwab US Broad (Stock) Market (SCHB)

8% SPDR Barclays 1-3 Month T-Bill (BIL)

20% Schwab Intermediate US Treasury (SCHR)

17% Schwab International Equity (SCHF)

3% Schwab US REIT (SCHH)   5% SPDR Gold (GLD)

20% Schwab US Aggregate Bond (SCHZ)

Growth Allocation Using ETFs

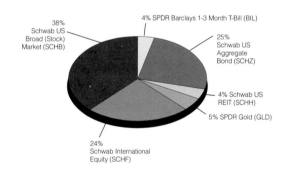

38% Schwab US Broad (Stock) Market (SCHB)

4% SPDR Barclays 1-3 Month T-Bill (BIL)

25% Schwab US Aggregate Bond (SCHZ)

4% Schwab US REIT (SCHH)

5% SPDR Gold (GLD)

24% Schwab International Equity (SCHF)

Conservative Allocation Using ETFs

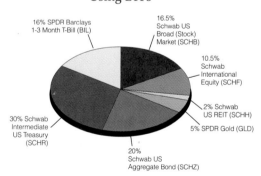

16% SPDR Barclays 1-3 Month T-Bill (BIL)

16.5% Schwab US Broad (Stock) Market (SCHB)

10.5% Schwab International Equity (SCHF)

2% Schwab US REIT (SCHH)

5% SPDR Gold (GLD)

30% Schwab Intermediate US Treasury (SCHR)

20% Schwab US Aggregate Bond (SCHZ)

CHART 14-2

Conclusion

Either index mutual funds or ETFs can be used to build a passive investor's Wealth and Retirement Portfolio. Either approach offers the relative certainty of matching their Model Portfolio's long term results. The differences between the two approaches are fairly small.

However, with ETFs, it is important to pay attention to both liquidity and leverage. Without sufficient liquidity – or by employing leverage – the anticipated index tracking may not be certain.

ETFs have become very popular over the past 10 to 15 years – primarily for their low cost and flexibility. However, for long-term investors as opposed to short-term traders, the ability to trade these funds during trading hours is of little advantage over time.

For those who choose actively managed mutual funds for some or all of their Wealth and Retirement portfolio, a portfolio of index funds or ETFs should be constructed and monitored as a benchmark for their portfolio's performance. It will provide the appropriate yardstick for their Model Portfolio's performance.

15

Identifying Consistently Superior Mutual Fund Managers

Introduction

Like many investors, you may be invigorated by the challenge of outperforming the index averages. Assembling a portfolio of mutual funds with superior managers at the helm offers the potential of higher returns and/or lower volatility than that of your benchmark (index) portfolio. This chapter lays out a uniquely successful approach to identifying many of those funds that have demonstrated success at consistently outperforming their targeted asset class.

"It is impossible to produce superior performance unless you do something different from the majority."
— John Templeton

Consistency

When evaluating actively managed mutual funds, one must look for those funds that have consistently added value to the index returns of the asset class within which they invest. The key word is consistently. This is where most analysis on whether actively managed mutual funds can beat the indexes falls short.

Anyone can look at one-year and three-year performance charts and point out those mutual funds that beat their relevant index. But without consistency over longer time periods it has questionable meaning with regard to predicting future superior performance. Of course even superior active funds are not going to outperform an appropriate index every year.

 As a long-term investor in actively managed mutual funds, you want a selection criteria that identifies mutual fund managers that have the highest likelihood of outperforming the asset class they are filling within your Wealth and Retirement Portfolio over a long period of time. There are two important criteria for this analysis:

- The Manager/Management Culture

- Performance over full market cycles

Investment Manufacturers

Unfortunately, many of the most recognizable names in the mutual fund industry are simply "Investment Manufacturers." Their primary goal is to gain market share and find as much "shelf space" as possible … in your portfolio. They are rewarded more for building their "AUM", an acronym for assets under management, than for their investment performance. In his book *The Battle for the Soul of Capitalism*, Vanguard Funds founder Jack Bogle declared that mutual fund companies had "gone from stewardship to salesmanship."

These fund manufacturers are all too often structured primarily to pump out a "new product" that raises sales. Such firms have a very large presence in the mutual fund industry. Warren Buffett says that "Size is the anchor of performance. There is no question about it". By this he means that the larger the AUM of a fund, the harder it is for them to outperform over time.

Artisans, Stewards of Capital

Some firms care more about their clients or fund shareholders than they do about building AUM. These "artisans" are a little harder to uncover, as they do not typically advertise in print or on TV. Artisans share many of the following characteristics.

<u>Owner Operators.</u> Many of the best artisan mutual fund companies are owned by the managers of their funds. When the manager of the fund owns the fund company, his interests are more aligned with his investors. Much of the artisan manager's net worth will likely be invested within his fund or within his fund family. Artisans tend to be very concerned with their reputation as stewards of their investors' capital.

<u>Investment Boutiques.</u> The best artisans are often specialist fund companies. They are focused on their own highly developed investment approach and completely ignore the flavor of the month in the fund industry. They are not trying to be all things to all people like the manufacturers, but instead work within their very special area of competence.

<u>Closing Their Funds.</u> An artisan will often close his fund to new investors when the fund gets too big to manage in the best interest of his shareholders.

<u>A Strong Firm Identity.</u> Most of the best artisans have a focused investment process or philosophy which can be seen across their typically small fund lineup. The stocks they invest in may change over time with their approach to value, but the philosophy behind their strategy does not. Rarely will you find

an artisan manager that excels using two or more different approaches.

Succession Planning is extremely important at these funds. In most cases, an artisan fund's track record is based on the reputation and experience of one particular fund manager. It is his excellent performance as a portfolio manager that drew in investors. Many of these superior fund managers are strongly motivated to see their fund continue to perform after they step down. To accomplish this, they hire very talented investment teams and personally train and guide them as they gain experience.

These new teams are immersed in the culture of the firm. In many such cases, the former lead manager stays on as an "adviser" to the fund. That way the new management team can build their own track record but under the guidance of the past manager and/or owner of the firm. The best mutual fund managers are obsessed with investing and are not only happy to stay involved, they couldn't imagine not doing it.

Full Market Cycle

Very few mutual funds offer a 20+ year track record to evaluate. Therefore, a method for identifying the truly superior mutual funds over a somewhat shorter time period is needed.

Recall the discussion of asset classes and Model Portfolios during the Great Depression (Chapter 10). It was stated that the only fair evaluation of a time period shorter than 20 years would be that of a full market cycle, i.e. one full bull market and one complete bear market. The same logic applies to the evaluation of mutual fund managers. Obviously, the more market cycles over which a fund manager can be evaluated relative to his or her target asset class the more confidence one has in the manager's results.

One particularly relevant argument for evaluating a fund's performance over a market cycle is that various styles of fund management tend to earn their rewards at different times within the cycle. Some managers do their best during the advancing half of the cycle and others are at their best during the declining part of the cycle. Therefore, beginning mid-cycle will unfairly penalize managers employing one style while benefiting managers with different styles.

The bottom line is simply this: funds cannot be considered "superior" until they have *proved* their ability to outperform their relevant benchmark over at least one full market cycle. The more full cycles of continuous outperformance by a manager, the more confidence you can develop in their ability to keep delivering superior long-term performance.

The Cream of the Crop

We will now introduce a group of mutual fund artisans that have delivered superior performance over at least one full market cycle and provide comparisons with their benchmarks through the end of 2011.

The "Face Off" charts presented in this chapter compare the full market cycle performance of proven superior mutual funds with that of their target asset class. The comparisons begin with the earliest bull market peak or bear market trough for which performance information on the fund is available.

The first funds presented are domestic equity funds that have outperformed over many full market cycles. As discussed in Chapter 2, the Russell 3000 Index is used as the benchmark for domestic stocks. Therefore, any domestic equity mutual fund or ETF will be measured in essence against the total U.S. stock market.

Stock Managers

The Sequoia Fund has been an outstanding fund since the 1970s. Our comparison covers a period of over 30 years.

The Sequoia Fund has had two sets of fund managers since its inception. Bill Ruane and Rick Cunniff, the founding managers, managed the fund successfully until 2005. They were true artisans that developed a very special culture at their fund. When Warren Buffett shut down his investment partnership in the early 1970s, he referred his clients to them. The new management team of Bob Goldfarb (1998) and David Poppe (2006) have proven themselves as worthy successors at Sequoia.

For the last full market cycle which includes the Financial Crisis (November 2007 through December 2011), Sequoia Fund produced a positive return of 10% while the Russell 3000 fell by 10%. For the prior full market cycle that included the dot com crash Sequoia Fund was up 101% while the Russell 3000 was up 20%. For the overall poor markets that have marked our time of uncertainty beginning in 2000 through the end of 2011, Sequoia has substantially outperformed the total U.S. stock market index.

Face Off: Sequoia vs Russell 3000

(April 1981-December 2011)

	Sequoia	Russell 3000
Advances & Declines		
Mar 2009 → Dec 2011* Recovery Started	85%	85%
Nov 2007 → Feb 2009 Financial Crisis	-41%	-51%
Oct 2002 → Oct 2007 Recovery & On to New Highs	64%	116%
Sep 2000 → Sep 2002 Dot Com Crash	23%	-44%
Sep 1998 → Aug 2000 Recovery & On to New Highs	10%	67%
Jul 1998 → Aug 1998 Asian Flu	-18%	-17%
Nov 1990 → Jun 1998 Recovery & On to New Highs	523%	353%
Jun 1990 → Oct 1990 Desert Storm War	-17%	-16%
Dec 1987 → May 1990 Recovery & On to New Highs	53%	68%
Sep 1987 → Nov 1987 87 Crash	-15%	-30%
Aug 1982 → Aug 1987 Recovery & On to New Highs	228%	260%
Apr 1981 → Jul 1982 Early 80s Recession	15%	-17%
Apr 1981 → Dec 2011 Total Gain	**4,988%**	**1,929%**
Annualized Gain	**13.6%**	**10.3%**

Officially this has not reached bull market status yet because the markets have not reached a new high. This will end up being an official bull market at that point if February 2009 remains the ultimate low.

Full Market Cycles

	Sequoia	Russell 3000
Nov 2007 → Dec 2011 Financial Crisis & Start of Recovery	10%	-10%
Sep 2000 → Oct 2007 Dot Com Crash & Following Bull Market	101%	20%
Jul 1998 → Aug 2000 Asian Flu & Following Bull Market	-9%	39%
Jun 1990 → Jun 1998 Desert Storm & Following Bull Market	418%	280%
Sep 1987 → May 1990 87 Crash & Following Bull Market	30%	18%
Apr 1981 → Aug 1987 Early 80s Recession & Following Bull Market	278%	200%

CHART 15-1

Like all of the equity funds that are highlighted in this chapter, the Sequoia Fund gained most of its outperformance in the DOWN part of the market cycle – the bear markets. This is very investor friendly as it creates a much smoother ride than a fund that outperforms in the up markets and underperforms in the down markets. This is a key characteristic especially when investing in uncertain times. Very few managers can outperform consistently in both up and down markets.

Review the Sequoia Fund's performance during all of its full market cycles (Chart 15-1). Pay special attention to the fund's ability to dampen downside volatility during bear markets. Sequoia outperformed the Russell 3000 Index in 5 out of 6 full market cycles.

The FPA Capital Fund was managed by Bob Rodriguez from its inception in 1984 through the end of 2009. In 2010 he handed the reigns over to Dennis Bryan and Rikard Ekstraud, his long-time assistant managers. He then took a one year sabbatical. He returned to FPA as a senior adviser at the beginning of 2011. FPA Capital's performance comparison with the Russell 3000 is shown in Chart 15-1. In the 1980s and 1990s FPA Capital sometimes outperformed in bull markets and sometimes in bear markets. Similarly to Sequoia the only underperformance was the one market cycle that included the tail end of the "tech bubble" in the late 1990s.

Face Off: FPA Capital vs Russell 3000
(September 1987-December 2011)

			FPA Capital	Russell 3000
Advances & Declines				
Mar 2009 → Dec 2011*	Recovery Started		122%	85%
Nov 2007 → Feb 2009	Financial Crisis		-47%	-51%
Oct 2002 → Oct 2007	Recovery & On to New Highs		122%	116%
Sep 2000 → Sep 2002	Dot Com Crash		9%	-44%
Sep 1998 → Aug 2000	Recovery & On to New Highs		43%	67%
Jul 1998 → Aug 1998	Asian Flu		-24%	-17%
Nov 1990 → Jun 1998	Recovery & On to New Highs		692%	353%
Jun 1990 → Oct 1990	Desert Storm War		-36%	-16%
Dec 1987 → May 1990	Recovery & On to New Highs		73%	68%
Sep 1987 → Nov 1987	87 Crash		-30%	-30%
Sep 1987 → Dec 2011	**Total Gain**		**1,820%**	**576%**
	Annualized Gain		**12.9%**	**8.2%**

Officially this has not reached bull market status yet because the markets have not reached a new high. This will end up being an official bull market at that point if February 2009 remains the ultimate low.

Full Market Cycles

			FPA Capital	Russell 3000
Nov 2007 → Dec 2011	Financial Crisis & Start of Recovery		18%	-10%
Sep 2000 → Oct 2007	Dot Com Crash & Following Bull Market		143%	20%
Jul 1998 → Aug 2000	Asian Flu & Following Bull Market		10%	39%
Jun 1990 → Jun 1998	Desert Storm & Following Bull Market		403%	280%
Sept 1987 → May 1990	87 Crash & Following Bull Market		21%	18%

CHART 15-2

Both of these funds' managers decided to take risk off the table a little early in that "bubble," but the move paid off handsomely during the following bear market (2000-2002). Each fund actually produced positive results while the benchmark lost half of its value. Both of these artisan funds have shown the ability to preserve capital far better than the index of the US stock market during bear markets. This is an ideal management strategy to employ in uncertain times.

The First Eagle Overseas Fund has been an outstanding international fund choice. The legendary Jean-Marie Evilard was the original manager from the fund's start in 1993. Jean-Marie was lead manager until his hand-picked successor, Matt McLennon, took the reins in 2008.

First Eagle Overseas has performed particularly well during the uncertain market period that began in 2000. For the last Full Market Cycle which includes the Financial Crisis, the fund produced a gain of 5% while the FTSE All World Ex-US Index was down 28%.

As discussed in Chapter 4, the FTSE All World Ex-US is used as the benchmark for international stocks. For the Full Market Cycle that included the dot com crash First Eagle was up 252% while our preferred international benchmark, the FTSE All World Ex-US index, gained 91%. This was outstanding outperformance over that period. (See Chart 15-3)

Face Off: First Eagle Overseas vs FTSE All World Ex US
(November 1994-December 2011)

		First Eagle Overseas	FTSE All World Ex US
Advances & Declines			
Mar 2009 → Dec 2011*	Recovery Started	54%	68%
Nov 2007 → Feb 2009	Financial Crisis	-32%	-57%
Oct 2002 → Oct 2007	Recovery & On to New Highs	208%	248%
Jan 2000 → Sep 2002	Dot Com Crash	14%	-45%
Oct 1998 → Dec 1999	Recovery & On to New Highs	43%	60%
May 1998 → Sep 1998	Asian Flu 2	-15%	-16%
Dec 1997 → Apr 1998	Recovery & On to New Highs	12%	15%
Aug 1997 → Nov 1997	Asian Flu 1	-8%	-12%
Mar 1995 → Jul 1997	Recovery & On to New Highs	47%	40%
Nov 1994 → Feb 1995	Interest Rates Rise	-4%	-9%
Nov 1994 → Dec 2011	**Total Gain**	**528%**	**137%**
	Annualized Gain	**11.3%**	**5.1%**

Officially this has not reached bull market status yet because the markets have not reached a new high. This will end up being an official bull market at that point if February 2009 remains the ultimate low.

Full Market Cycles

		First Eagle Overseas	FTSE All World Ex US
Nov 2007 → Dec 2011	Financial Crisis & Start of Recovery	5%	-28%
Jan 2000 → Oct 2007	Dot Com Crash & Following Bull Market	252%	91%
May 1998 → Dec 1999	Asian Flu & Following Bull Market	22%	34%
Aug 1997 → Apr 1998	Asian Flu	2%	2%
Nov 1994 → Jul 1997	Recovery	41%	27%

CHART 15-3

Like Sequoia and FPA Capital, First Eagle Overseas gained its outperformance in the DOWN markets. The Fund believes that their first responsibility is return OF capital before considering return ON capital. First Eagle Overseas has never underperformed in a bear market. However, it has only once outperformed in a bull market. Yet, First Eagle outperformed in 4 of 5 full market cycles and substantially outperformed the All World Ex-U.S. Index over the entire time period analyzed.

Bond Managers

The PIMCO Total Return Fund, continuously managed by Bill Gross since 1987, has proven it can consistently outperform the Aggregate Bond Index over full market cycles. The fund posted similar downside U.S. returns as the index but outperformed in every bond bull market. This points out an important distinction between bond funds and stock funds. In the bond world, many of the best managers outperform in UP markets and have similar returns to the Index in DOWN markets. The PIMCO Total Return Fund has outperformed in each of the last three bond market cycles.

Face Off: PIMCO Total Return vs US Total Bonds
(February 1994-December 2011)

			PIMCO Total Return	US Total Bonds
Advances & Declines				
Nov 2008→ Dec 2011*	Recovery & On to New Highs		37%	30%
Apr 2008→ Oct 2008	Financial Crisis		-4%	-4%
Aug 2003→ Mar 2008	Recovery & On to New Highs		32%	26%
Jun 2003 → Jul 2003	Iraq War		-4%	-4%
Jul 1994 → May 2003	Recovery & On to New Highs		117%	104%
Feb 1994 → Jun 1994	Interest Rates Rise		-6%	-5%
Feb 1994 → Dec 2011	**Total Gain**		**215%**	**195%**
	Annualized Gain		**6.6%**	**6.2%**

Officially this has not reached bull market status yet because the markets have not reached a new high. This will end up being an official bull market at that point if February 2009 remains the ultimate low.

Full Market Cycles				
Apr 2008→ Dec 2011	Financial Crisis & Start of Recovery		31%	25%
Jun 2003 → Mar 2008	Iraq War to Financial Crisis		27%	22%
Feb 1994 → May 2003	Interest Rates Rise to Iraq War		105%	93%

CHART 15-4

The <u>Loomis Sayles Bond Fund</u> has been continuously managed by Dan Fuss since 1991. Kathleen Gafney joined as co-manager in 1997. This fund is more venturesome than the U.S. Aggregate Bond Index and it has paid off handsomely over time.

It invests in a wider variety of low grade corporate bonds and bank debt. It also invests abroad when the opportunity warrants it. By far the most notable example of this fund's volatility was seen in the financial crisis. Loomis Sayles Bond was down 25% while the Index was only down 4%. Over most other bear markets Loomis

Sayles was quite competitive. Even with the substantial decline in 2008, the fund still outperformed the index since the beginning of the financial crisis in the full market cycle that includes the financial crisis. In each of the other full market cycles Loomis Sayles far outperformed the U.S Aggregate Bond Index. In the bond world where small differences in return are significant, this degree of outperformance is extraordinary. (See Chart 15-5)

Face Off: Loomis Sayles Bond vs US Total Bonds
(February 1994-December 2011)

			Loomis Sayles Bond	US Total Bonds
Advances & Declines				
Nov 2008→	Dec 2011*	Recovery & On to New Highs	73%	30%
Apr 2008→	Oct 2008	Financial Crisis	-25%	-4%
Aug 2003→	Mar 2008	Recovery & On to New Highs	56%	26%
Jun 2003 →	Jul 2003	Iraq War	-3%	-4%
Jul 1994 →	May 2003	Recovery & On to New Highs	156%	104%
Feb 1994 →	Jun 1994	Interest Rates Rise	-8%	-5%
Feb 1994 →	**Dec 2011**	**Total Gain**	**339%**	**195%**
		Annualized Gain	**8.6%**	**6.2%**

Officially this has not reached bull market status yet because the markets have not reached a new high. This will end up being an official bull market at that point if February 2009 remains the ultimate low.

Full Market Cycles

Apr 2008→	Dec 2011	Financial Crisis & Start of Recovery	29%	25%
Jun 2003 →	Mar 2008	Iraq War to Financial Crisis	52%	22%
Feb 1994 →	May 2003	Interest Rates Rise to Iraq War	136%	93%

CHART 15-5

Follow the Manager

We discussed earlier in this chapter, the importance of the superior manager and the artisan culture that they create. In some cases, a proven fund manager will leave their fund company and strike out on their own. This can be a great opportunity. Two recent examples are Charles Akre and Jeffrey Gundlach. Each of these two outstanding fund managers applied their skills for another company before starting their own funds. In order to analyze their skill, one must analyze both their current fund's track record and also the track record of their prior fund. This allows one to evaluate how they have performed over their entire tenures.

By piecing together Akre's track record at FBR Focus then tacking on his track record at his current fund, AKRE Focus, one can get a true picture for his investing skill. For the last full market cycle which includes the financial crisis, Akre as a manager gained 6% while the Russell 3000 Index was down 10%. For the full market cycle that included the dot com crash Akre was up a full 228% while the Russell 3000 was up only 20%. For the poor market conditions that have existed since the beginning in 2000, Akre has substantially outperformed.

Face Off: Akre vs Russell 3000

(July 1998-December 2011)

		Akre	Russell 3000
Advances & Declines			
Mar 2009→ Dec 2011*	Recovery Started	95%	85%
Nov 2007→ Feb 2009	Financial Crisis	-46%	-51%
Oct 2002 → Oct 2007	Recovery & On to New Highs	202%	116%
Sep 2000 → Sep 2002	Dot Com Crash	9%	-44%
Sep 1998 → Aug 2000	Recovery & On to New Highs	52%	67%
Jul 1998 → Aug 1998	Asian Flu	-23%	-17%
Jul 1998 → Dec 2011	**Total Gain**	**294%**	**51%**
	Annualized Gain	10.7%	3.1%

*Officially this has not reached bull market status yet because the markets have not reached a new high. This will end up being an official bull market at that point if February 2009 remains the ultimate low.

Full Market Cycles

Nov 2007→ Dec 2011	Financial Crisis & Start of Recovery	6%	-10%
Sep 2000 → Oct 2007	Dot Com Crash & Following Bull Market	228%	20%
Jul 1998 → Aug 2000	Asian Flu & Following Bull Market	16%	39%

CHART 15-6

Jeff Gundlach managed the TCW Total Return fund with great success from 1993 to 2009. In April of 2011, he began his own firm – Doubleline Capital. By piecing together his returns at TCW to those of Doubleline Total Return one can evaluate his entire performance starting with the bear market in bonds in 1994. Gundlach has outperformed the U.S. Aggregate Bond Index in all three full market cycles. (Bond Indexes are actually more difficult to outperform than stock indexes).

Face Off: Gundlach vs US Total Bonds
(February 1994-December 2011)

		Gundlach	US Total Bonds
Advances & Declines			
Nov 2008 → Dec 2011*	Recovery & On to New Highs	54%	30%
Apr 2008 → Oct 2008	Financial Crisis	-1%	-4%
Aug 2003 → Mar 2008	Recovery & On to New Highs	27%	26%
Jun 2003 → Jul 2003	Iraq War	-1%	-4%
Jul 1994 → May 2003	Recovery & On to New Highs	114%	104%
Feb 1994 → Jun 1994	Interest Rates Rise	-7%	-5%
Feb 1994 → Dec 2011	**Total Gain**	302%	195%
	Annualized Gain	7.8%	6.2%

Officially this has not reached bull market status yet because the markets have not reached a new high. This will end up being an official bull market at that point if February 2009 remains the ultimate low.

Full Market Cycles

Apr 2008 → Dec 2011	Financial Crisis & Start of Recovery	53%	25%
Jun 2003 → Mar 2008	Iraq War to Financial Crisis	27%	22%
Feb 1994 → May 2003	Interest Rates Rise to Iraq War	99%	93%

CHART 15-7

Hybrid Funds

During uncertain investment climates many investors may want to broaden their search for exceptional funds. As we have seen, the stock market is subject to high levels of volatility. Hybrid funds offer a mixture of stocks and fixed income. Hybrid funds may cushion overall volatility if they replace one or more stock funds within your Wealth and Retirement Portfolio. The best artisan hybrid fund managers have substantially outperformed during down markets while still providing excellent long-term results.

FPA Crescent is a hybrid fund that has been managed since its inception in 1993 by Steven Romick. The fund has underperformed the Russell 3000 domestic stock market index in every bull market and outperformed in every bear market over its existence. In high flying stock markets like the late 1990s, FPA Crescent will most likely lag far behind. However, markets where stock picking prowess, risk controls, and investing latitude are rewarded, this fund proved its worth. FPA Crescent has taken far less risk than the Russell 3000 over the last three full market cycles, yet produced a much higher overall return.

Face Off: FPA Cresent vs Russell 3000
(July 1998-December 2011)

			FPA Cresent	Russell 3000
Advances & Declines				
Mar 2009 → Dec 2011*	Recovery Started		56%	85%
Nov 2007 → Feb 2009	Financial Crisis		-25%	-51%
Oct 2002 → Oct 2007	Recovery & On to New Highs		96%	116%
Sep 2000 → Sep 2002	Dot Com Crash		34%	-44%
Sep 1998 → Aug 2000	Recovery & On to New Highs		8%	67%
Jul 1998 → Aug 1998	Asian Flu		-14%	-17%
Jul 1998 → Dec 2011	**Total Gain**		**220%**	**51%**
	Annualized Gain		9.1%	3.1%

Officially this has not reached bull market status yet because the markets have not reached a new high. This will end up being an official bull market at that point if February 2009 remains the ultimate low.

Full Market Cycles

Nov 2007 → Dec 2011	Financial Crisis & Start of Recovery		17%	-10%
Sep 2000 → Oct 2007	Dot Com Crash & Following Bull Market		163%	20%
Jul 1998 → Aug 2000	Asian Flu & Following Bull Market		-7%	39%

CHART 15-8

Matthews Asia Growth & Income Fund is an international hybrid fund focusing on Asia. Investors can certainly include such regional funds as a portion of their overall commitment to international stocks. Like FPA Crescent, the fund will also invest in fixed income and focuses on risk controls. Over the last three full market cycles, Mathews Asia Growth & Income has performed exceedingly well while taking much less risk than the international index. As a piece of an international allocation it offers a very attractive risk/reward profile.

Face Off: Matthews Asia Growth & Income vs FTSE All World Ex US
(November 1994-December 2011)

		Matthews Asia Growth & Income	FTSE All World Ex US
Advances & Declines			
Mar 2009 → Dec 2011*	Recovery Started	63%	68%
Nov 2007 → Feb 2009	Financial Crisis	-38%	-57%
Oct 2002 → Oct 2007	Recovery & On to New Highs	200%	248%
Jan 2000 → Sep 2002	Dot Com Crash	28%	-45%
Oct 1998 → Dec 1999	Recovery & On to New Highs	70%	60%
May 1998 → Sep 1998	Asian Flu 2	-17%	-16%
Dec 1997 → Apr 1998	Recovery & On to New Highs	1%	15%
Aug 1997 → Nov 1997	Asian Flu 1	-26%	-12%
Mar 1995 → Jun 1997	Recovery & On to New Highs	36%	40%
Nov 1994 → Feb 1995	Interest Rates Rise	-7%	-9%
Nov 1994 → Dec 2011	**Total Gain**	**418%**	**137%**
	Annualized Gain	**10.1%**	**5.1%**

Officially this has not reached bull market status yet because the markets have not reached a new high. This will end up being an official bull market at that point if February 2009 remains the ultimate low.

Full Market Cycles

Nov 2007 → Dec 2011	Financial Crisis & Start of Recovery	1%	-28%
Jan 2000 → Oct 2007	Dot Com Crash & Following Bull Market	283%	91%
May 1998 → Dec 1999	Asian Flu & Following Bull Market	41%	34%
Aug 1997 → Apr 1998	Asian Flu	-25%	2%
Nov 1994 → Jul 1997	Recovery	27%	27%

CHART 15-9

Other Candidates

Each of the following mutual fund managers has also proven his
ability to outperform his target asset class over at least one full
market cycle, while bettering the performance of the target asset
class over his entire management tenure. This is not a complete list
of qualifying funds. (Be aware that many of the best known, best
performing fund managers over one-, three- and five-year periods
fail this test and that many other potentially superior mutual fund
managers have not proved themselves over a long enough career).

Asset Class	Mutual Fund	Manager
U.S. Stocks	Yacktman Fund	Donald Yacktman, Stephen Yacktman, Jason Subotky
U.S. Stocks	Longleaf Partners	O-Mason Hawkins, John B. Buford, G. Staley Cates
U.S. Stocks	Royce Special Equity	Charles R. Dreifus
Hybrid	T. Rowe Price Capital Appreciation	David R. Giroux
Hybrid	Greenspring Fund	Charles Carlson
International Stock (Emerging Markets)	Oppenheimer Developing Markets[1]	Justin Leverenz

---

[1] Oppenheimer Developing Markets invests primarily in the Emerging Markets therefore it should onrepresent a smaller portion of an investors international fund allocation within a Wealth and Retirem
Portfolio.

Asset Classes Best left to Indexing

5-Year U.S. Treasury Bond Asset Class

Intermediate-term government bond funds come closest to capturing the risks and rewards of the 5-year U.S. Treasury bond asset class used throughout this book. Individual funds within this group may vary their criteria to differentiate their fund from the others within the group. Typical of such distinguishing characteristics are:

- Lengthening or shortening the average maturity of the bonds within the fund

- Including government agency securities or mortgage notes issued or guaranteed by quasi-government agencies such as FNMA or GNMA (mortgage backed securities)

- Adding illiquid securities and/or options, futures or warrants to be purchased and

- Adopting exotic or leveraged strategies in the hope of boosting yields and returns.

With this asset class, it may be preferable to focus on reliability. Plain vanilla intermediate government bond funds with a very low fee structure, such as the index funds discussed in Chapter 14, are a better option than higher risk and uncertain strategies for most investors. Reaching for a one-half percent total return advantage over the index (if you were to be very successful over time) may not be worth the risk or time involved.

In fact, if your portfolio is large enough to allow it, purchases of U.S. Treasury bonds either directly or through a broker may be more desirable than a mutual fund for this asset class.

Gold

The allocation to gold in the Model Portfolios is best delivered by bullion itself or a vehicle that buys it on your behalf. If you do not want to buy and store gold bullion, the GLD ETF is a good alternative.

Conclusion

Superior mutual fund managers are available to your Wealth and Retirement Portfolio. These managers have proved themselves where it counts - over several full market cycles. Choosing superior fund managers to fill out your asset allocation policy offers the highest probability of providing long-term performance which outdistances that of your benchmark (index) portfolio.

This chapter describes a unique method of uncovering superior actively managed mutual funds – those that have *consistently* rewarded their shareholders. In <u>Beyond Stocks,</u> published in 1997, John Merrill introduced this methodology and highlighted 10 U.S. stock mutual fund managers. The first full market cycle after the book was published began in July of 1998. In the three full market cycles that followed, the cumulative returns of each of the funds highlighted in <u>Beyond Stocks</u> are shown below ranked by cumulative returns over the entire time period (July 1998 to December 2011).

In addition, the total return of the U.S. stock market as represented by the Russell 3000 index is included. As a group, the highlighted funds in 1997 substantially outperformed the domestic stock benchmark over three full market cycles.

1. Acorn Fund (Ralph Wanger) : +211%
2. Heartland Value Fund (Bill Nasgovitz) : +181%
3. Mutual Qualified Fund (Michael Price) : +134%
4. Kaufmann Fund (Auriana and Utsch) : +121%
5. Longleaf Partners Fund (Mason Hawkins) : +90%
6. Baron Asset Fund (Ron Baron) : +73%
7. Davis NY Venture Fund (Shelby Davis/Chris Davis) : +66%
8. FPA Paramount Fund (Bill Sams) : +57%
9. **Russell 3000 : +51%**
10. Brandywine Fund (Foster Friess) : +38%
11. PBHG Growth (Gary Pilgrim) : N/A (Shut down in 2004 because of operational issues)

16

The Not-So-Secret Key Ingredient to Investing in Uncertain Times

Introduction

Whether investing in index funds, ETFs or actively managed funds, many investors are disappointed by the returns they make from their investments. The culprit is often market timing. They buy when it feels good to invest (after a bull market has produced much of its gains) and sell when it feels scary (late in a bear market). The solution is to select an investment strategy you can rely upon and then stay the course. This discipline may be the most important ingredient in attaining long term investment success.

"Our stay-put behavior reflects our view that the stock market serves as a relocation center at which money is moved from the active to the patient."

— Warren Buffett

Have you ever sat on a river bank, one with a fast-moving current and scattered rapids? Perhaps you threw pieces of bark or branches into the water. If your "ship" made it to the main current - off it went - caught in the major force of the river. It bobbed and weaved wildly, but its course was undeniable. You had no doubt where it was heading.

If your ship did not make the main current, it may have been caught in swirling eddies, or in dead-end side streams or even in the calm water near the edge. Not being part of the major force of the river, your ship might end up anywhere, while the major rush of the river passed it by.

We want our *investment* ships in the main current. The ride may be spirited, but we know where we're going, and we know we'll get there.

Prediction Deficit

An asset allocation policy is arguably the most predictable approach to long-term investing and thus the best antidote to uncertainty. In Chapter 9, a set of Model Portfolios employing specific asset allocation policies were introduced that spanned the range from low volatility with lower rewards to high volatility with higher rewards.

Therein lies a fundamental truth about intelligent asset allocation using reliable asset classes. Higher long-term returns go hand-in-hand with larger declines during bear markets. Yet, it *seems* sensible to go for the high returns of an aggressive portfolio allocation during bull markets and to retreat to a more conservative allocation during bear markets. But this falsely assumes that one can perfectly anticipate the major movements of the markets!

Financial publications and various market gurus oblige this desire by offering market forecasts that appear logical and well founded based upon analysis of economic and market data. The problem is consistency. *No publication or market analyst has ever consistently forecast the direction of the economy or the market!*

Examples could not only fill a book, they could fill a reference library!   One-time gurus such as Joe Granville, Elaine Garzarelli and Marty Zweig had their 15 minutes of fame with uncanny market calls only to fall to earth on subsequent lousy (and costly) ones.

Even Ned Davis, one of the better known market timers, is candid about the limitations of technical analysis. He once gave a seminar in which he used a series of indicators to argue that the Dow Jones Industrial Average would rise by 1000 points over the next 12 months. After a short break, he returned to the podium and used another set of indicators to argue that the Dow would shed 1000 points in the coming 12 months. "The point being," says Davis, "that at any time there are enough indicators to make a credible case in either direction" (*Smart Money*, March, 1997).

Market timing comes in many different forms, but the long-term results are always the same. Whether based on technical indicators, fundamental values or market sentiment (moods), they just rob you of your valuables: *time* and *compounding*.

Peter Lynch put it in different terms: "Far more money has been lost by investors in preparing for corrections, or anticipating corrections, than has been lost in the corrections themselves."

Performance Chasing

Chasing hot mutual funds or asset classes is the bane of other investors. In a report titled *The Plight of the Fickle Investor*, Morningstar stated, "We found that investors across all fund types - both stocks and bonds - have paid a price for being fickle. Swapping in and out of funds wouldn't be so bad if we were actually good at it. But...we're not. Instead of buying low and selling high, we do the opposite. So rather than checking fund prices first thing each morning, let's show some restraint, develop an investment plan, and stick to it. As Warren Buffett said, 'Inactivity strikes us as intelligent behavior', If it works for him..."

This same phenomenon can be witnessed by investors who invest in index funds or ETFs. Even though these products offer market certainty, low costs and fees and the possibility of an average or lower tax bite, these attributes of an index strategy disappear if you attempt to achieve short-term advantages by rotating among the asset classes. This adds elements of both market timing and performance chasing.

This is not just a subtle change or enhancement; it is an entirely different strategy. As Gus Sauter, President of Vanguard Funds, said, "(Asset class) rotating is like betting, pure and simple. It's silly to choose a strategy that guarantees market returns and then use it in a way that risks loss."

Full Recovery of Market Declines

 It cannot be over emphasized that there have been no permanent losses in the well-diversified portfolios outlined in Chapter 9, only temporary declines that have been fully recovered during the following bull market. This is the ultimate reward of patient, disciplined investing.

On the other hand, the market gains that are not captured by being out of the market during a bull market, may be lost forever. The investor, who misses the gains of his asset allocation by sitting in cash, may not get a second chance. The market may continue going up and never come back down to the point where that investor exited the markets. In this scenario, the investor has permanently impaired his long-term results.

Experience Builds Patience

Investing is not easy, and the most difficult part of all is in mastering our own emotions. Let's listen in again on another part of Louis Rukeyser's insightful interview on April 28, 1995, with

Phil Carret, the voice of 77 years of investment management experience:

RUKEYSER: "What is the most important thing that you have learned about investing over the past three-quarters of a century?"

CARRET: "Patience."

RUKEYSER: "What do you think of this stock market today?"

CARRET: "I think it is dangerous at current levels. There's a lot of froth on the bloom. I think we're in for maybe something like 1987 when the market went down 500 points in one day...But in the long run...the market will recover, and people who buy the right stocks and sit on them are going to do very well."

RUKEYSER: "What do you do, given your experience, when you think there may be too much froth, when you think there may be a major correction, even a crash? Do you sell all your stocks?"

CARRET: *"No, I really don't do anything."*

Conclusion: Don't Just Sit There - Do Nothing!

It appears that the great philosopher Blaise Pascal could have been discussing investment philosophy in 1670 when he said, "I have discovered that all human evil comes from this, man's being unable to sit still in a room."

 Your asset allocation policy will control your risks - let it! Any market timing or performance chasing you attempt to enhance returns and/or reduce setbacks has a very high probability of doing exactly the opposite - lowering your long-term returns and increasing the risk that you will fall well short of your retirement income objective.

Your asset allocation policy is much more powerful and predictable than any ad hoc system of investing! Let it work for you.

17

Protecting Your Portfolio from Inflation and Taxes

Introduction

Investors must always keep a watchful eye not only on their stated investment returns, but also on economic/governmental factors which directly add to, or more likely, take away from their quoted returns. These include: changes in currency value, cost-of-living and tax policy. Real wealth is only increased when calculated after inflation and after taxes.

> *"The only return that matters is the return after inflation and taxes."*
>
> — Sir John Templeton
> (Founder of Templeton Funds)

Government Economic Policy

Within every country, economic forces and government policies greatly impact the wealth and well-being of its citizens. Communism destroyed both the national economy and the wealth of its people (who were not politically connected). As is also clear, poor governmental policies in democracies such as Argentina have devastated the average citizen while entrenching the very wealthy. These extreme examples demonstrate the potency of government and the economic policies they pursue.

In the U.S., it was poor governmental policies that deepened both the Great Depression and the Great Inflation of the 1970s. In the 1930s, the government raised interest rates as the economy worsened and shrank the money supply by one-third. In addition, congress passed the Smoot-Hawley Act which raised tariffs significantly and greatly eroded world trade.

In the late 1960s, our government financed the war in Vietnam *and* President Johnson's Great Society social programs – all without increasing taxes. They were paid for with "printing-press dollars" created out of thin air. This was the primary source of the horrid inflation of the 1970s.

It is therefore critical that each U.S. citizen be vigilant as to the economic policies being pursued. Are they consistent with a stable currency? Will they foster only modest cost-of-living changes? Will they allow individuals to save and invest after taxes? Will they encourage rising standards of living for all citizens?

Nominal and Real Returns

We live in a world of *nominal returns*, returns that are not adjusted for inflation. Your bank quotes interest rates this way, mutual funds advertise performance nominally, the U.S. government offers most Treasury bonds and T-bills at nominal rates and so forth.

Yet *real returns*, those adjusted for inflation, are far more important to your Wealth and Retirement Portfolio. *There is no creation or addition to wealth without increased purchasing power.* And, in the same vein, the further in the future your proposed retirement dollars are needed, the more the amount of your retirement income in nominal dollars becomes misleading. The purchasing power of those dollars is all that counts.

Inflation's Slow Burn

Investors should fear inflation. It is a particularly insidious financial disease. Inflation attacks the corpus (principal) and the productive effort (yield or interest) of an investment at the same time. It is not only cumulative, it compounds like an interest-bearing account in reverse. After 30 years of retirement with inflation at 3%, a retiree will need $250 to buy what $100 did when he retired. In other words, both your portfolio and retirement income must grow by 150% just to purchase the goods and services it did when retirement began.

Unfortunately, inflation is not reflected on either your bank or brokerage statements. It grows unseen like a cancerous tumor. A graphic analogy of how inflation exacts its price is that of the proverbial "frog on the stove." As you have probably heard, if you place a frog in a pot of water on the stove and turn on the burner so that the water slowly heats to a boil, the frog will stay in the pot - even with full opportunity to hop out - until he boils to death. The slow incremental burn never rings an alarm to get out until it is too late.

Lower Inflation, Lower Returns

From the early 1980s to the early 2010s, U.S. fiscal and monetary policies brought the inflation rate down from the extremely high level of the 1970s. The average inflation rate in the 1980s and 1990s was approximately 3.5%. Beginning in the 2000s, the inflation rate came down even further. If this trend continues investors may view the returns on their investments as being disappointing even if they delivered real returns that were consistent with historical real return averages.

For example, assume inflation were to average only 1.5% over the next 20 years. Now assume that U.S. Large Cap stocks average a real return of 6.5% annually over that same period. This is consistent with long-term trends discussed on page 38. Taken together, the real return of 6.5% plus inflation of 1.5% would equal a nominal average return of 8.0% per year. Because of the much higher average nominal return of the past 40 years, this result would probably *feel* very low. Yet this return would build wealth and support retirement objectives in line with historical results.

Higher Inflation Ahead?

Many economists and investors are concerned that both fiscal policy and monetary policy in the United States since 2008 are laying the groundwork for much higher inflation at some point in the second decade of this century (2012 – 2020).

The source of this concern is the massive increase in the U.S. Federal Reserve's balance sheet from under $1 trillion in 2008 to almost $3 trillion in the following three years through policies referred to as "quantitative easing." The fear is that once the U.S. economy fully recovers after the Great Recession, these excess reserves will be available to our banking system. Under our fractional reserve system, many times this excess $2 trillion could flood into the economy with significant inflationary impact.

Federal Reserve chairman, Ben Bernanke, has stated on numerous occasions including testimony before Congress that he believes that the excess reserves can be safely withdrawn as the economy improves – before any major inflationary impulse begins. Yet many economists are skeptical as there are no historical precedents for such actions.

Quantitative easing policies are not unique to the U.S. Federal Reserve.   Central banks from Japan to Great Britain to the European Central Bank have also greatly expanded their balance sheets since the Financial Crisis in 2008. In some cases this was to offset *deflation*, in others to liquefy their banking systems. In each case, the real risks at hand were deemed greater than the potential risk of much greater inflation down the road.

Certainly these policies have softened the impact and consequences of the Great Recession and Financial Crisis. Time will tell if these policies come back to haunt the U.S. economy with much higher rates of inflation. This is one of the major uncertainties currently hanging over investors' heads.

The good news is that the Model Portfolios developed in Chapter 9 performed quite well during our last severe bout of printing money and inflation in the 1970s. They would likely see long term investors through once again.

The Big Bite from Taxes

This discussion of taxation is necessarily general as the tax code is thousands of pages long. This section will merely give the reader an overview of selected areas of taxation that affect investments.

Since the inception of the income tax in 1913, the U.S. government's tax policy has significantly impacted investor returns. Yet not all forms of returns are taxed the same. Interest (from bonds, bills and money market accounts) is termed "ordinary income." Dividends (from stocks) currently have a preferential tax rate, although it is set to expire at the end of 2012. Municipal bond interest is typically not ordinary income and is usually free of federal taxes. Capital gains from the sale of stocks are subject to unique rules and tax rates.

For individual investors, ordinary income is taxed progressively, beginning at 10% of taxable income and topping out at the largest marginal rate, 35%, in 2012. The maximum effective rate had recently been as high as 39.6% (1993-2001) and as low as 28% (1987-1990).

Capital gains taxes have also jumped around quite a bit. Through 2012, the capital gains on equities held more than one year have recently been taxed at a maximum rate of 15%. This rate had effectively been 28% from 1978-1982, 20% from 1982-1986, 33% from 1987-1989, 28% from 1990-1996, 20% again to 2003 and 15% through 2012.

Quite obviously, taxes tend to materially reduce the returns from all financial assets except municipal bonds. However, municipal bonds typically yield less than comparable taxable bonds yield to compensate for their tax-favored nature.

Tax Strategies

Individual taxpayers need to carefully consider the impact of taxes in their long-term planning. The starting point should be to divide their investment assets into taxable accounts and tax deferred accounts. Taxable accounts are subject to the rules of taxation on capital gains, interest and dividends discussed above.

Tax deferred accounts such as 401(k) plans, pensions, IRAs, etc. are a wonderful planning tool. While inside these accounts, all taxes on gains, interest and dividends are deferred. Taxes are paid on amounts distributed from these plans in the year of the withdrawal. Almost all distributions are subject to ordinary income tax rates. This is a distinct advantage for those who do not need income today from their investments. A multitude of studies have shown that this deferral of taxes increases after-tax returns, even when considering the full taxation of the proceeds on being paid out. Obviously, the longer the deferral of tax, the greater the tax advantage.

As a general rule, the best tax strategy for working individuals with upper tax brackets above 15% is to make full use of tax deferred accounts. This means that they should contribute the maximum possible to the 401(k), thrift, 403(b), etc. plans that are offered by their employer.

For investors with taxable investment accounts, there are a variety of strategies they can employ:

- Hold capital assets at least one-year before selling to get long-term capital gain treatment (short-term gains are subject to ordinary income tax rates)
- Offset capital gains with capital losses in a specific tax year (the law allows aggregating of capital gains and losses)
- Choose municipal bond funds for longer term liquidity needs
- Sell a mutual fund with a sizeable tax loss and replace it with a similar fund in order to "harvest" the tax loss

For investors with both taxable and tax deferred accounts; these additional strategies apply:

- Put investments that generate significant ordinary income into tax deferred accounts – REITs (Chapter 5), bond funds, higher yielding equity mutual funds
- Utilize taxable accounts for equity funds that will generate mostly long-term capital gains

Tax Strategies for Mutual Funds

All that Matters

Sir John Templeton, the founder of the highly regarded Templeton Group of funds, was fond of saying throughout his career that "the only return that counts is the after-tax, after-inflation return on your investments." There is more than an element of truth in his insight. Whatever you pay Uncle Sam from your investments will not add to your wealth nor will it supplement your retirement income.

Therefore, it makes good sense to be aware of tax mistakes to avoid as well as smart moves to take advantage of within your Wealth and Retirement Portfolio.

Year-End Distributions

In order to eliminate double taxation, each mutual fund must distribute the net capital gains it has realized throughout the year, either by the end of December or at the end of October. The date chosen is at the option of each fund.

If you purchase a mutual fund in a taxable account just prior to its making a large taxable distribution, you may wish you had waited to purchase it...or had purchased this mutual fund in a tax deferred account (IRA, IRA rollover, 401(k), etc.). This is an area where you must be proactive. Mutual funds will rarely alert you as to either the exact date or the amount of such distributions.

Tax Efficiency

If some or all of your Wealth and Retirement Portfolio is in a taxable account, pay attention to a fund's tax efficiency. This is the relationship between a fund's pre-tax returns and its after-tax returns. The pinnacle of tax efficiency would be having your after-tax returns equal your pre-tax returns. No taxes due. A mutual fund that delivered such a stellar result would be 100% tax efficient.

Many mutual funds - including some of the higher performing ones - are more than 85% tax efficient.

Of course, a poor performing mutual fund would not jump into consideration just because it is highly tax efficient. (A "zero" total return with no tax due is 100% tax efficient!) In the same vein, a great fund should not be totally discounted just because it is somewhat below average in this area. (Optimally, you could place such a fund in a tax-deferred pocket within your portfolio.)

Tax efficiency discussions are often included in both Morningstar's and Value Line's individual mutual fund evaluations. They provide theoretical examples based upon the highest tax rates.

Another variation of this theme is the introduction of tax managed index funds. Vanguard Funds, Charles Schwab and others have introduced index mutual funds specifically designed to be highly tax efficient. The underlying strategy of these funds is to hold onto each security unless forced to do so. If a sale is necessary, first sell the higher cost shares and, when possible, sell losing security positions to offset the gains. This approach is certainly worth considering for index funds within taxable accounts.

Taxable Yields

If you have an IRA, 401(k) or other such tax-deferred account within your Wealth and Retirement Portfolio, attempt to place as many of your higher yielding mutual funds into this account. Bond funds and equity mutual funds with a value focus, i.e. those that produce high levels of dividend and interest income, would typically be higher yielding than other types of funds.

The reason for this focus on yields is two-fold. First, the total tax bite on interest income currently exceeds that of long-term capital gains and dividends. Second, mutual fund managers cannot reduce the tax bill on interest and dividend income through strategies such as realizing offsetting capital losses discussed above.

Selling Funds

When you have a need to sell some portion of any one of several mutual funds within your taxable portfolio, check the tax basis of each mutual fund relative to its current value. In other words, what percentage of the sales price will be taxable to you? All else being equal, sell the fund with the lowest tax hit (highest tax basis).

If a portion of a particular fund must be sold, consider selling shares from the lot(s) with the highest cost basis. This will minimize the tax bite on the sale.

Once you build up significant tax-deferred gains within a particular mutual fund, think twice before selling it. This is particularly true if you are merely switching to a different but similar fund within your taxable portfolio. You will have fewer dollars - after taxes - to invest in the new fund.

Giving some thought to the tax aspects of investing and actively employing the tax strategies above should enhance the return that counts – the return after taxes.

Conclusion

Inflation directly reduces the wealth generation (buying power) from nominal returns. In a period of low inflation, investors should expect lower nominal returns. Conversely, in a period of high or rapidly rising inflation, investors need higher nominal returns to offset inflation's impact. Fortunately, the Model Portfolios – with their specific combinations of asset classes – have performed well in both environments.

Tax planning is an essential element of good investing as taxes can take a big bite out of returns. The first step is to know (or work with someone who knows) current tax policies very well – and how they impact your personal situation.

The second step is to become familiar with tax reduction *strategies* such as offsetting capital gains with capital losses, tax harvesting mutual fund losses, side stepping year-end mutual fund distributions, fully utilizing tax deferred accounts and so forth.

Finally, be proactive. The tax world – like the investment markets – is in continuous motion. Opportunities come and go. You – or someone you work with – must be current with both and be prepared to make those changes which will maximize your real return.

18

The "One Decision" Strategy that Works

Introduction

Employing an investment adviser may be the best way for many investors to implement the ideas outlined in this book. A professional manager can assure the discipline, expertise and time required to execute your plan.

> "The emergence of this new profession of disinterested investment [advisers], who have no allegiance or alliances and whose only job is to judge a security on its merits, is one of the most constructive and healthy developments of the last half century."

> — Bernard Baruch (1957)

The Force is with You

Do you know someone who has gone to a health spa?

Many people who just can't seem to eat right or exercise with consistency in their normal life seem to fall right in step with the spa's healthy lifestyle.

Why do these programs work? They succeed because it takes only one decision - the decision to do it. Once you have made that decision, paid the price, arranged the travel, you don't have to make any more decisions. No temptations. No hesitations. You avoid the noise of the 1,000 and more distractions and excuses that come your way in your everyday "normal" life.

You surrender both your normal distractions and normal surroundings to be totally enmeshed in a culture that is completely supportive of your higher goal. Everything is lined up for success - the facility (all good stuff, no bad stuff), the staff (positive, goal-oriented, professionally competent) and your fellow campers ("we're all in this together") make it almost impossible to fail.

Best of all, you do it gladly. You know it works, it's what you want and this is the way to make sure it gets done, even if it costs more than doing it on your own.

One Decision

In the same sense, choosing a money manager can be your one decision that makes everything in this book work for you. The management firm can be your Health Spa of Finance. The professional money manager provides knowledge, confidence and experience in the development and execution of your personal financial game plan, as well as the ongoing management of your investments. No more hesitations to plan your financial future or temptations to tamper with a well-thought-out investment policy. The end result - peace of mind.

Candidates for a Money Manager

In Chapter 13 we looked at the types of investors who would be good candidates for investing with index funds/ETFs and those that would be a better fit with actively managed mutual funds. The differences revolved around their attitude and expectations from investing. Let's look at who might be a good candidate for hiring a personal money manager.

Issue	*Candidate for Money Manager*
Guidance	"I want personal consulting and guidance to make sure my objectives, asset allocation policy and related financial issues are on track."
Service	"I would like a complete package of account services that include consolidated performance reports, accounting, tax preparation, rebalancing and special services such as income distributions and tracking."
Discipline	"I'm not sure that I will have the discipline on my own to stay with my asset allocation policy or my mutual fund strategy during substantial changes in market conditions."

CHART 18-1

If you decide to hire an investment professional to manage some or all of your Wealth and Retirement Portfolio, understand that, at a minimum, you are still responsible for evaluating and selecting the appropriate investment policy that is right for you. The manager then selects the mutual funds, ETFs (or individual securities) that best execute your plan.

Your investment manager should help you assemble your financial information to determine where you stand currently. He should also help clarify your future needs and objectives. And most importantly, your investment adviser should reinforce and personalize the market education you have received from this book; particularly in reaching the all-important asset allocation decision.

However, in the end, the investment policy that is the most appropriate trade-off between long-term returns and degree of market setbacks along the way is *your* call. There is no escaping from the fact that this is your money, that the long-term returns will greatly affect your retirement or wealth and that only you know what degree of temporary loss (it will seem like a permanent loss when it occurs) you can tolerate without emotional trauma.

Once the asset allocation policy is in place, *you* can relax and turn over the reins to your investment manager. You don't have to watch the market on a day-to-day basis, and you are relieved of the stress and strain of having to make your own investment selections and placing your own transactions. You can focus on your own activities - even travel with confidence - because the management firm is there overseeing your portfolio and financial plan on a daily basis.

What to Look For in an Investment Adviser

There are many important considerations when evaluating a prospective adviser with which to work.

- *Professional.* Is this money manager a full-time professional with an established counseling practice?

  A true professional should be registered with the Securities and Exchange Commission (SEC) by filing a form "ADV." Ask for a copy, review it thoroughly. It will detail all the nuts and bolts of the adviser's practice as well as his principal investment philosophy and experience.

- *Quarterback.* Will this money manager help you evaluate your entire Wealth and Retirement Portfolio - including the parts *not* to be directly managed (for instance: your 401(K) account, company stock options, and/or other illiquid investments) - in order to help formulate and adhere to the overall plan?

- *Asset Allocation.* Will the adviser help you establish your asset allocation? Will the adviser agree to stay within its boundaries? (Maintaining your portfolio's structure is fundamental to achieving the expected long-term returns with the anticipated degree of periodic setbacks in market values.) Will the adviser provide a suitable benchmark for performance comparisons?

- *Performance.* A good money manager is a craftsman, building an <u>audited</u> performance record that has unique risk and reward characteristics. Review this track record for accounts with similar objectives to your own. How has the firm performed relative to its benchmark? This is the true test of the manager's investment skills.

- *Fee-Only.* Does the adviser charge an annual fee for managing your account or does he receive per-transaction commissions? The adviser's method(s) of compensation should be clearly set forth in the firm's ADV filing (see above).

  Fee-only managers are professionals whose interest is identical to your own - to maximize the value of your account relative to your risk parameters. There's neither pressure to buy or sell investments nor a conflict of interest in making investment recommendations. When advisers are paid in other ways, either by the investment funds or by selling you products, a clear conflict of interest arises.

- *Cost Conscious.* Other costs can vary widely when looking at investment advisers. Ask your prospective adviser if he or she buys the least expensive share class of each mutual fund available for his clients. It is important that potential adviser is not incentivized to pick funds based on how much they pay him which creates a conflict of interest.

  There is a trade-off to hiring your own money manager. The typical fee charged by a money manager is approximately one percent of the money under his direct management per year. Some investment advisers will charge as little as one-half of one percent per year and others as much as two percent per year or more. Be aware that costs and quality do not necessarily go hand in hand.

- *Enjoyable Relationship.* This should be entered into as a long-term relationship. Make sure it feels right from the beginning. Is there a spirit of trust, cooperation and mutual respect?

If the results of this initial investigation are satisfactory to you, then ask the adviser for at least two referrals of long-term clients of the firm that share similar characteristics and objectives to your own. Call them. Ask them to speak candidly of their relationship with the adviser. Ask them to address the adviser's strengths and weaknesses. Referrals are not enough though as we will see in the next section.

Protecting Yourself from Investing in a Madoff Scheme

Most investment advisers do not hold their client's assets. Instead the assets are placed with an independent, third party custodian. This arrangement is the single biggest safeguard for investors to prevent getting caught in a Madoff type Ponzi scheme.

The arrangement that most Ponzi artists employ is referred to as "self-custody". This is where client assets are held by the adviser himself or a brokerage company that he owns. With self custodied accounts, the adviser has direct access to your money and his clients have no way of independently verifying the accuracy of his account statements. A Ponzi scheme only works if the adviser is able to take money from his victim's accounts without them being able to see it in their statements.

As stated above, the vast majority of advisers utilize independent, third party custodians such as Fidelity or Charles Schwab. In these arrangements, the client opens an account with say Charles Schwab Institutional and gives the adviser a Power of Attorney to trade the account. Charles Schwab will send statements directly to the client. The numbers on the Schwab statement should always match up with the exact same positions on the advisers report. The client can check their account online through Schwab at any time. This provides an important safety check for a client which goes a long way toward eliminating the possibility of getting trapped in a fraudulent "Madoff" scheme.

(You can read more about this on the SEC's website www.sec.gov.)

Counseling and Communication

In our health spa analogy at the beginning of this chapter, it was pointed out that one of the reasons the spa works is the completely supportive atmosphere, including staff and fellow campers. Good money management firms will put a lot of effort into providing you with high-quality support for your Wealth and Retirement Portfolio objectives.

This is one area where there are significant differences between money management firms.

Your management firm should prepare simple, consolidated reports that illustrate your asset allocation, your individual holdings, your current-period performance and your historical performance. Your fee will be clearly shown and netted against your gross return to reflect your bottom-line return. Your net returns are then compared to those of your benchmark (see Chapter 14). This provides you with a measuring tool for both returns and setbacks.

This is important. Whether by phone or in person, conversations with your adviser should include complete discussions of just how your account is doing relative to its objectives. With appropriate benchmarks, you are not guessing, you are not at the mercy of your manager's presentation...*you know!*

Professional money managers prepare detailed quarterly reports to keep you informed of their current market insights and the reasoning behind any changes that have either just occurred or are anticipated within your portfolio. The quality of these reports varies widely.

Some money managers add interim client reports and special individual correspondence to highlight specific activity within the firm or within your individual portfolio.

Many of the more established advisers organize quarterly or annual meetings in which clients are invited to participate. This is an informative way to hear your money manager's broader views as well as interact with other clients of the firm and hear their questions and comments. This can be very positive reinforcement. (For those who cannot attend, a recording and/or of the presentation may be offered on their website).

It is very important that you take advantage of all the counseling and communication that your money manager offers. It is both informative and supportive.

Conclusion

A qualified money manager is an excellent strategy for those who want a third-party to enforce the discipline of their investment policy. There are a myriad temptations to alter a well-thought-out, long-term asset allocation *at just the wrong time. A* professional's services may be a better choice than either utilizing index funds or developing your own portfolio of managed funds. In addition, your investment adviser can customize your strategy to focus on increasing the returns and/or decreasing the risks within your Wealth and Retirement Portfolio.

There are a myriad of ancillary services the best advisers provide in terms of monitoring, executing, and reporting on accounts that can truly make the experience your health spa of finance....even in uncertain times.

> *"We have striven throughout to guard the student against over emphasis upon the superficial and the temporary...this over emphasis is at once the delusion and the nemesis of the world of finance."*
> — Benjamin Graham and David Dodd,
> *Security Analysis*, 1934

Action Summary

Here is a simple summary of the important points in this book. Understanding and acting upon them will help assure your investment success... even in these uncertain times.

Motivate yourself to invest better. Understand that the rate of return you achieve on your investments may be the single most important determinant of the retirement income available to you.

Organize your retirement portfolio - all of it - on one page. Begin thinking of it as an entity in itself, not a collection of separate investments. Purchase financial software that makes this much easier.

Educate yourself as to the long-term returns that asset classes and combinations of asset classes are likely to provide. Also, appreciate the interim fluctuations in market values that are a part of each class. Be armed and prepared *not to act*!

Select an asset allocation that is appropriate for your Wealth and Retirement Portfolio - the right combination of long-term return and fluctuation in market values that is satisfying and livable for you.

Choose your strategy for investing within the asset allocation you select. Index funds? Actively managed funds? Your own personal money manager? One of these is the best choice for you. Size yourself up based on your attitude and expectations from investing.

Research and uncover those few superior mutual fund managers experienced in the styles appropriate to your objective (actively managed fund strategy) – OR - select a professional money manager to do this for you.

Stay put with your asset allocation and investment strategy. To get the benefits of a well-thought-out investing program, you still need the patience and discipline to stay the course - either on your own or with help from an adviser.

Rebalance your asset allocation periodically.

Build Wealth and....Have a Great Retirement!

Appendix

Note: Charts in the Appendix are the letter A (for Appendix) followed by the chapter number in which the chart is introduced or to which it is referred. A hyphen follows these two digits which is followed by the individual chart number.

How Much Retirement Income Will Your Current Tax-Sheltered Account Provide?

(Inflation-Adjusted, Retirement Income as a Percentage of Your Current Tax-Sheltered Retirement Account)

Years to Retirement	Annual Rates of Return							
	5%	6%	7%	8%	9%	10%	11%	12%
0	4.3%	4.9%	5.5%	6.2%	7.0%	7.8%	8.6%	9.4%
10	5.2%	6.6%	8.1%	10.1%	12.4%	14.9%	18.0%	21.8%
15	5.7%	7.6%	9.8%	12.8%	16.4%	20.7%	26.2%	33.1%
20	6.3%	8.7%	11.9%	16.2%	21.8%	28.8%	38.0%	50.4%
25	6.9%	10.1%	14.4%	20.6%	28.9%	40.0%	55.3%	76.6%
30	7.6%	11.7%	17.4%	26.1%	38.4%	55.6%	80.4%	116.4%
35	8.4%	13.5%	21.1%	33.1%	50.9%	77.2%	116.8%	176.9%
40	9.2%	15.5%	25.5%	41.9%	67.6%	107.2%	169.8%	269.0%

CHART A1-1

Note: In order to estimate future income from a portfolio, it is necessary to make certain assumptions:
- Inflation is assumed to be 3.0% per year (both before and after retirement).
- Retirement income will be adjusted annually by the increase in inflation.
- Retirement income will be paid out for 30 years before the investment principal is depleted.

Example: Assume you currently have $300,000 in a tax-deferred account, such as a Rollover IRA, 401(k), profit sharing plan or deferred annuity. Further assume you are 15 years away from beginning to take retirement distributions from this account (shaded on chart). Based on the assumptions noted, your maximum level of retirement income will be determined by the rate of return from your investments both before and after retirement. Assume your investment return averages 7% per year (shaded on chart). At this rate of return, your maximum retirement income will be $29,400 ($300,000 x 9.8%) per year *in today's dollars* for 30 years. A year-by-year illustration of this example is shown on Chart A1-2.

This chart is designed to illustrate the impact on your retirement income of merely changing the rate of return on your current investment portfolio. Changing your rate of return has a dramatic impact on your available retirement income. In the example above, a 5% annual rate of return reduces retirement income to only $17,100 per year in current dollars, whereas increasing the rate of return to 9% results in an annual retirement income of $49,200 per year in present value dollars.

Tax Sheltered Net Worth

Lump Sum:	$300,000
Years to Retirement:	15
Inflation Rate:	3%
Pre-Retirement Total Return:	7%
Post-Retirement Total Return	7%

Years Before and After Retirement	Accumulated Wealth	Retirement Income	
1	$321,000	N/A	
2	343,470	N/A	
3	367,513	N/A	
4	393,239	N/A	
5	420,766	N/A	
6	450,219	N/A	
7	481,734	N/A	
8	515,456	N/A	
9	551,538	N/A	
10	590,145	N/A	
11	631,456	N/A	
12	675,657	N/A	*$46,027 equates to $29,400 in present dollars at 3% inflation. Each annual retirement income distribution increases by 3%; however, the buying power of each year's income remains $29,400 in present dollars.*
13	722,954	N/A	
14	773,560	N/A	
15	$827,709	$46,027	
1	838,241	47,408	
2	848,089	48,830	
3	857,160	50,295	
4	865,358	51,804	
5	872,575	53,358	
6	878,697	54,958	
7	883,598	56,607	
8	887,145	58,305	
9	889,190	60,055	
10	889,577	61,856	
11	888,136	63,712	
12	884,682	65,623	
13	879,018	67,592	
14	870,929	69,620	
15	860,186	71,708	
16	846,540	73,860	
17	829,722	76,075	
18	809,445	78,358	*30 Years of Retirement Distributions*
19	785,398	80,708	
20	757,246	83,130	
21	724,630	85,623	
22	687,162	88,192	
23	644,425	90,838	
24	595,972	93,563	
25	541,320	96,370	
26	479,951	99,261	
27	411,309	102,239	
28	334,794	105,306	
29	249,765	108,465	
30	155,529	111,719	

	$ 51,345	*Final Distribution - Principal Depleted*

CHART A1-2

10% SALARY DEFERRAL

What Percentage of Your "Final Salary"
Will Your 401(k) Replace?
(Your Retirement Income as a Percentage of Your Final Compensation)

Years to Retirement	Annual Rates of Return							
	5%	6%	7%	8%	9%	10%	11%	12%
10	4.9%	5.9%	7.0%	8.4%	9.9%	11.6%	13.5%	15.6%
15	7.5%	9.3%	11.4%	13.9%	16.9%	20.2%	24.3%	29.0%
20	9.8%	12.3%	15.4%	19.2%	23.9%	29.3%	36.0%	44.0%
25	13.3%	17.3%	22.4%	28.8%	37.0%	47.2%	60.3%	76.5%
30	16.2%	21.7%	28.9%	38.4%	50.9%	67.8%	88.6%	116.5%
35	19.5%	26.8%	36.8%	50.4%	69.1%	94.0%	128.8%	175.7%
40	22.7%	32.1%	45.4%	64.1%	90.9%	129.7%	184.4%	261.3%

CHART A1-3

Assumptions:
- Annual rate of return is for both "years to retirement" *and* 30 years after retirement.
- Annual Inflation: 3.0% (both before and after retirement)
- Annual Salary Increases: 1.0% (over inflation)

Example: You anticipate you will retire in 20 years (shaded on chart). You and your employer together will set aside 10% of your growing annual salary each year. (Your salary is assumed to grow 1.0% per year above inflation.) If your investments average a 9% rate of return (shaded on chart) both before and after retirement, your investments from the 20 years of salary deferral will replace 23.9% (shaded on chart) of your *final* salary. Your retirement income will fully adjust for changes in the Consumer Price Index (CPI), that is the income paid out to you during your retirement will rise each year by the inflation rate. The income will last 30 years at which time all of the investment principal would be consumed. (See opposite page for a full illustration of this example.)

This chart is designed to illustrate the impact on your retirement income of merely changing the rate of return on your 401(k) investments.

Retirement Income as a % of Final Compensation

Compensation:	$25,000	Inflation Wage Adjustment:	3%
Contribution Level:	10%	Portfolio Rate of Return (Pre-Retirement):	9%
Merit Wage Adjustment:	1%	Portfolio Rate of Return (Post-Retirement):	9%

Years Before and After Retirement	Compensation	Plan Contribution	Plan Accumulation/ Retirement Fund	Retirement Income	
1	$26,000	$2,600	$ 2,834	0	
2	27,040	2,704	6,036	0	
3	28,122	2,812	9,645	0	
4	29,246	2,925	13,701	0	
5	30,416	3,042	18,249	0	
6	31,633	3,163	23,340	0	
7	32,898	3,290	29,026	0	
8	34,214	3,421	35,368	0	
9	35,583	3,558	42,430	0	
10	37,006	3,701	50,282	0	
11	38,486	3,849	59,002	0	
12	40,026	4,003	68,675	0	
13	41,627	4,163	79,393	0	
14	43,292	4,329	91,258	0	
15	45,024	4,502	104,378	0	
16	46,825	4,682	118,876	0	
17	48,698	4,870	134,883	0	
18	48,698	4,870	134,883	0	Each annual
19	50,645	5,065	152,543	0	retirement income
20	$52,671	$5,267	$172,013	$12,081	distribution increases
1			175,050	12,444	by 3%; however, the
2			177,988	12,817	buying power of each
3			180,805	13,202	year's income remains
4			183,480	13,598	at 23.9% of final
5			185,987	14,006	compensation.
6			188,300	14,426	
7		Increasing/(Decreasing)	190,389	14,859	
8		Value of	192,219	15,304	
9		Retirement Fund	193,756	15,764	
10			194,957	16,236	
11			195,780	16,724	
12			196,175	17,225	
13			196,089	17,742	
14			195,462	18,274	
15			194,231	18,822	
16			192,325	19,387	
17			189,666	19,969	
18			186,168	20,568	
19			181,738	21,185	
20			176,274	21,820	30 Years of
21			169,664	22,475	Retirement
22			161,784	23,149	Distributions
23			152,501	23,844	
24			141,667	24,559	
25			129,122	25,296	
26			114,688	26,055	
27			98,173	26,836	
28			79,368	27,641	
29			58,040	28,471	
30			33,939	29,325	

$ 6,789   Final Distribution - Principal Depleted

CHART A1-4

How Much Retirement Income Will Your Current
After-Tax Account Provide?

(Inflation-Adjusted, Retirement Income as a Percentage of Your Current After-Tax Retirement Account)

Years to Retirement	Annual Rates of Return							
	5%	6%	7%	8%	9%	10%	11%	12%
0	3.5%	3.8%	4.2%	4.6%	5.1%	5.5%	6.1%	6.6%
10	3.6%	4.3%	5.1%	6.0%	7.0%	8.1%	9.5%	11.0%
15	3.7%	4.6%	5.6%	6.8%	8.2%	9.8%	11.9%	14.2%
20	3.8%	4.8%	6.1%	7.7%	9.6%	11.9%	14.8%	18.3%
25	3.9%	5.1%	6.7%	8.7%	11.2%	14.4%	18.5%	23.6%
30	4.0%	5.4%	7.4%	9.9%	13.1%	17.4%	23.2%	30.5%
35	4.1%	5.7%	8.1%	11.2%	15.4%	21.1%	29.0%	39.4%
40	4.2%	6.1%	8.8%	12.6%	18.0%	25.5%	36.2%	50.9%

CHART A1-5

Note: In order to estimate future income from a portfolio, it is necessary to make certain assumptions:
- Inflation is assumed to be 3.0% per year (both before and after retirement).
- Retirement income will be adjusted annually by the increase in inflation.
- Retirement income will be paid out for 30 years before the investment principal is depleted.

Example: You assume you will retire in 25 years (shaded on chart). You currently have a Wealth and Retirement Portfolio of $300,000. If your portfolio averages a 10% rate of return (shaded on chart) both before and after retirement, your after-tax retirement income (distributions from your portfolio) will have the same purchasing power as 14.4% (shaded on chart) of today's $300,000 throughout your retirement (30 years). In other words, your retirement income from your current nest egg is the equivalent of $43,200 per year (14.4% x $300,000) in today's dollars after taxes. (See opposite page for a full illustration of this example.)

This chart is designed to illustrate the impact on your retirement income of merely changing the rate of return on your current investment portfolio.

Non-Tax Sheltered Net Worth

Lump Sum:	$300,000
Years to Retirement:	25
Inflation Rate:	3%
Tax Rate:	30%
% Taxable (Accumulation):	100%
Pre- and Post-Retirement Total Return:	10%
Pre- and Post-Retirement After-Tax Return:	7%

Years Before and After Retirement	Accumulated Wealth	Retirement Income	
1	$ 321,000	N/A	
2	343,470	N/A	
3	367,513	N/A	
4	393,239	N/A	
5	420,766	N/A	
6	450,219	N/A	
7	481,734	N/A	
8	515,456	N/A	
9	551,538	N/A	
10	590,145	N/A	
11	631,456	N/A	
12	675,657	N/A	
13	722,954	N/A	
14	773,560	N/A	
15	827,709	N/A	
16	885,649	N/A	
17	947,645	N/A	
18	1,013,980	N/A	
19	1,084,958	N/A	
20	1,160,905	N/A	
21	1,242,169	N/A	
22	1,329,121	N/A	*$90,542 equates to $43,200 in present dollars. Each annual retirement income distribution increases by 3%; however, the buying power of each year's income remains $43,200 in present dollars.*
23	1,422,159	N/A	
24	1,521,710	N/A	
25	$1,628,230	$ 90,542	
1	1,648,948	93,258	
2	1,668,318	96,056	
3	1,686,163	98,937	
4	1,702,289	101,906	
5	1,716,487	104,963	
6	1,728,529	108,112	
7	1,738,171	111,355	
8	1,745,148	114,696	
9	1,749,172	118,136	
10	1,749,933	121,681	
11	1,747,098	125,331	
12	1,740,304	129,091	
13	1,729,161	132,964	
14	1,713,250	136,953	
15	1,692,116	141,061	
16	1,665,272	145,293	
17	1,632,189	149,652	*30 Years of Retirement Distributions*
18	1,592,301	154,141	
19	1,544,996	158,766	
20	1,489,618	163,528	
21	1,425,456	168,434	
22	1,351,751	173,487	
23	1,267,682	178,692	
24	1,172,367	184,053	
25	1,064,858	189,574	
26	944,137	195,262	
27	809,107	201,119	
28	658,591	207,153	
29	491,325	213,368	
30	305,949	219,769	
	$ 101,004	*Final Distribution - Principal Depleted*	

CHART A1-6

Measures of Risk

Risk Profile is an investor's tool, not an academic measurement, for portraying the long-term risks of an asset class or portfolio. It takes into consideration the two primary characteristics of risk as *felt* by long-term investors: the worst-case decline in market value (major bear market) and the normal cyclical decline in market value (average bear market).

The number of bear market declines to be evaluated is determined by dividing by 5 the total number of years being studied. (Fractions of one-half or over add one additional decline to the study.) For example, in the 1972-2011 period of study (40 years), the eight most severe declines in market value are included (40 ÷ 5 = 8).

The rationale for dividing by five is simply that the total U.S. stock market has incurred one major decline *on average* about every five years. These declines do not operate on a predictable cycle, and therefore some five-year periods have no major declines and some five-year periods have more than one major decline. See the Historical Risk/Reward Chart 6-1 to visually see this illustrated for the S&P 500.

Declines, recoveries and advances are measured from calendar month-ends to subsequent calendar month-ends. (This lines up with the timing of brokerage and custodial valuations, i.e. month-end statements.) The end of a decline is established when a recovery restores the entire market value temporarily lost in the decline. All calculations are made on a total return basis without consideration of taxes or costs.

The most significant decline in the period of study is dubbed the worst bear market decline. On Chart 6-1, the worst decline for the S&P 500 in the 1972-2011 period is the decline that began in October, 2007 and ended in March, 2009. The S&P 500 fell a full <51%> during that "worst" bear market decline.

All the major declines (the eight most severe declines in this period of study) are averaged together to determine the average cyclical decline to which an investor was exposed. On Chart 6-1, the average cyclical decline of the S&P 500 in the 1972-2011 period was <31%>.

Standard deviation is a common measure of the volatility of annual returns. The standard deviation is defined as $s = \{[(r_1 - r_A)^2 + (r_2 - r_A)^2 + \ldots (r_n - r_A)^2]/n\}^{\frac{1}{2}}$, where $r_1, r_2 \ldots r_n$ are the individual yearly returns and r_A is the average, or *mean* of the yearly returns (s^2 is called the *variance*): if yearly returns follow a normal distribution, popularly known as the *bell-shaped curve*, then about two-thirds of the time the asset will have a return equal to the mean plus or minus one standard deviation. That is, the return on the asset will be within one standard deviation of its average, or mean, about two thirds of the time. About 95 percent of the time, the return on the asset will be within two standard deviations of its mean.

Example of Standard Deviation "Predictions"

Suppose that the average of all the annual returns from an investment over a 20-year period of study is 10%[1]. Further assume that this investment produced a standard deviation of 18.5% for this 20-year period. The standard deviation for this investment predicts the following:

- *13 of the 20 annual returns likely fell within the range of -8.5% to 28.5%*, the average annual return of 10% plus or minus one standard deviation

$$(10\% \pm 18.5\%)$$

- *19 of the 20 annual returns likely fell within the range of -27% to 47%*, the average annual return of 10% plus or minus two standard deviations

$$[10\% \pm (2 \text{ times } 18.5\%)]$$

---

[1] This is not the compounded average annual return from this investment, it is simply the arithmetic *mean* of all 20 of its annual returns.

- *1* annual return may be lower than *-27.0% or higher than 47.0%*

Standard deviation has one distinctive advantage—its precision. Academics and market commentators like the fact that any historical set of returns can produce this precise, annual measurement of volatility to match up with an investment's annual return.

Standard Deviation's Limitations

From an investor's viewpoint, standard deviation does have several insurmountable shortcomings as the measure of an asset class's risk, i.e. the intensity of its market declines.

- *Omission of Worst Case.* In the eyes of many investors, the most significant risk of an investment is defined by, "What's the worst that can happen?" A major handicap of standard deviation is that it leaves out the worst case. Over the long term, the standard deviation calculation will not predict or illustrate the very worst "bear market" decline that the investor will likely face.

Annual Risks vs. Total Risk. Standard deviation measures volatility in calendar year units. This has the effect of hiding or downplaying the real risks incurred. For example, in calculating the standard deviation for the S&P 500 index, a *positive* annual return is entered for 1987—the year of the crash! Is this an accurate portrayal of the risk that unfolded to investors in that year? Standard deviation also fails to prepare investors for the cumulative effect of back-to-back declines like 1973-1974.

Historical Risk/Reward charts are a better yardstick for illustrating the risk faced by a long-term investor within an asset class. On display are all the major market declines from beginning to end, regardless of calendar year starts and stops, as this is what the investor feels as his monthly brokerage statements arrive.

Model Portfolio Guidelines

Certain guidelines were adopted in order to prevent any model from being too lopsided toward any one particular asset class. These guidelines are:

- No asset class can represent more than 50% of a model portfolio (to ensure appropriate diversification).

- Every qualifying asset class must be represented in each model (except in the 100% Stocks Model Portfolio).

- International stocks may not exceed 50% of the stock portion of any model portfolio (approximately their total proportion of world markets).

- REITs may not exceed 5% of any model portfolio (approximately four times their total proportion of the domestic stock market).

Virtually every combination of domestic stock asset classes, 5-year Treasury bonds and 30-day T-bills that met the guidelines above was tested. The returns assumed a reinvestment of all dividends, interest and capital gains. The goal was to find the most favorable combination of the seven asset classes that satisfied the objectives set out for each model portfolio.

If more than one asset allocation met the rate-of-return objective and produced an identical level of risk, the portfolio with the most even distribution of asset classes was selected as the model.

All of the results of this study may be duplicated using the databases identified in Chart 7-1.

Simple Model Portfolio: Moderate
(September 1929 through February 1937)

Illustrates annual gains/declines by asset class and annual rebalancing back to 50% Stocks, 40% Bonds, 10% Cash.

Year			50% Stocks	40% Bonds	10% Cash	Nominal Value of Total Portfolio	Value of US $ Relative to 9/1/29	Real Value of Total Portfolio
1929	1-Sep		$500,000	$400,000	$100,000	$1,000,000	$1.00	$1,000,000
	Gain/<loss>		<158,160>	14,400	1,600	<142,160>		
	31-Dec		341,840	414,400	101,600	857,840	$1.01	$866,840
1930	1-Jan	(Rebalance)	$428,920	$343,136	$85,784	$857,840		
	Gain/<loss>		<113,870>	19,559	2,059	<92,252>		
	31-Dec		315,050	362,695	87,843	765,588	$1.07	$825,630
1931	1-Jan	(Rebalance)	$382,794	$306,235	$76,559	$765,588		
	Gain/<loss >		<167,710>	<11,637>	842	<178,504>		
	31-Dec		215,084	294,598	77,401	587,083	$1.17	$711,561
1932	1-Jan	(Rebalance)	$293,542	$234,833	$58,708	$587,083		
	Gain/<loss>		<23,037>	30,059	587	7,609		
	31-Dec		270,505	264,892	59,295	594,692	$1.29	$794,074
1933	1-Jan	(Rebalance)	$297,346	$237,877	$59,469	$594,692		
	Gain/<loss>		185,782	2,022	178	187,982		
	31-Dec		483,128	239,899	59,648	782,674	$1.29	$1,041,110
1934	1-Jan	(Rebalance)	$391,337	$313,070	$78,267	$782,674		
	Gain/<loss>		3,099	29,742	157	32,998		
	31-Dec		394,436	342,811	78,424	815,672	$1.26	$1,064,181
1935	1-Jan	(Rebalance)	$407,836	$326,269	$81,567	$815,672		
	Gain/<loss>		191,993	19,576	163	211,732		
	31-Dec		599,829	345,845	81,730	1,027,404	$1.22	$1,308,496
1936	1-Jan	(Rebalance)	$513,702	$410,962	$102,740	$1,027,404		
	Gain/<loss>		178,008	21,781	205	199,994		
	31-Dec		691,710	432,742	102,946	1,227,398	$1.21	$1,547,506
1937	1-Jan	(Rebalance)	$613,699	$490,959	$122,740	$1,227,398		
	Gain/<loss>		38,467	2,455	0	40,921		
	31-Dec		652,166	493,414	122,740	1,268,320	$1.20	$1,583,625

Average Annual Return over 90 Months: 2.7% (nominal) 5.2% (real)

CHART A10-1

Important Disclosure Information

John Merrill is the founder of Tanglewood Wealth Management, Inc. an SEC registered investment adviser located in Houston, Texas. Please remember that different types of investments involve varying degrees of risk. Therefore, it should not be assumed that future performance of any specific investment, investment product, or investment strategy (including the investments and/or investment strategies referenced in this book), or any of the book's non-investment related content, will be profitable, prove successful, or be applicable to any individual's specific situation. No reader should assume that the book serves as the receipt of, or a substitute for, personalized advice from Mr. Merrill and/or Tanglewood Wealth Management, Inc. or from any other investment professional. Should a reader have any questions regarding the applicability of any portion of the book content to his/her individual situation, the reader is encouraged to consult with the professional advisers of his/her choosing.

All model portfolio returns and returns of the underlying components include the reinvestment of all dividends (total return) and do not reflect the impact of taxes or fees. Performance information is based on data obtained from public sources believed to be reliable; however, the author does not guarantee the completeness or accuracy thereof.

Notes on Appendix Charts

The Retirement Distribution charts in the Appendix assume a hypothetical initial starting value of $1,000,000 and annual returns of the Moderate Balanced Portfolio. The initial income distribution rate shown on each chart is applied to the accumulated portfolio value at the end of each period and annually adjusted thereafter for inflation.

Moderate Balanced Portfolio

Maximun 40-Year "Real" Retirement Income

Initial Portfolio: $1,000,000   Initial Income: $51,000 (5.1% of Original Portfolio)

	The Numbers You See				The Numbers You Feel	
Year	The Portfolio is Deleted After 40 Years of Paying Increasing Retiree Distributions	Retiree's Annual Distributions — Increasing Annually with the Full Change in Inflation	CPI: Annual Inflation Rate %	CPI: Cumulative Inflation%	The Real Value of this Portfolio is Fairly Stable at First —then Declines Steadily	Retiree's Annual Distributions in Real $ (Adjusted for Inflation)
1972	$1,093,200	$51,000	3.4%	3.4%	$1,057,151	$51,000
1973	1,012,568	55,488	8.8	12.5	899,980	51,000
1974	880,444	62,258	12.2	26.2	697,457	51,000
1975	990,087	66,622	7.0	35.1	732,933	51,000
1976	1,068,080	69,826	4.8	41.6	754,384	51,000
1977	1,051,844	74,554	6.8	51.2	695,810	51,000
1978	1,094,255	81,286	9.0	64.8	663,914	51,000
1979	1,188,392	92,105	13.3	86.8	636,334	51,000
1980	1,282,853	103,526	12.4	109.9	611,133	51,000
1981	1,183,798	112,781	8.9	128.7	517,665	51,000
1982	1,300,216	117,146	3.9	137.5	547,390	51,000
1983	1,356,748	121,597	3.8	146.6	550,279	51,000
1984	1,347,571	126,400	4.0	156.3	525,789	51,000
1985	1,598,307	131,166	3.8	166.0	600,963	51,000
1986	1,849,093	132,648	1.1	169.0	687,490	51,000
1987	1,840,772	138,498	4.4	180.8	655,489	51,000
1988	1,925,145	144,619	4.4	193.2	656,516	51,000
1989	2,083,171	151,344	4.7	206.9	678,840	51,000
1990	1,885,292	160,591	6.1	225.6	578,982	51,000
1991	2,066,115	165,505	3.1	235.6	615,674	51,000
1992	1,972,049	170,305	2.9	245.3	571,082	51,000
1993	2,074,726	174,988	2.8	254.8	584,736	51,000
1994	1,902,949	179,660	2.7	264.3	522,375	51,000
1995	2,094,368	184,224	2.5	273.5	560,680	51,000
1996	2,102,155	190,340	3.3	285.9	544,681	51,000
1997	2,164,832	193,576	1.7	292.5	551,545	51,000
1998	2,242,424	196,692	1.6	298.8	562,261	51,000
1999	2,282,642	201,964	2.7	309.5	557,407	51,000
2000	2,101,224	208,810	3.4	323.4	496,282	51,000
2001	1,838,327	212,047	1.6	330.0	427,562	51,000
2002	1,580,791	217,093	2.4	340.2	359,116	51,000
2003	1,658,701	221,175	1.9	348.5	369,862	51,000
2004	1,588,556	228,385	3.3	363.1	343,038	51,000
2005	1,457,046	236,196	3.4	378.9	304,235	51,000
2006	1,403,247	242,195	2.5	391.1	285,743	51,000
2007	1,282,514	252,077	4.1	411.1	250,921	51,000
2008	842,579	252,304	0.1	411.6	164,700	51,000
2009	734,908	259,166	2.7	425.5	139,850	51,000
2010	557,030	263,054	1.5	433.4	104,434	51,000
2011	$297,943	$270,840	3.0%	449.2%	$54,253	$51,000

SPEND-IT-ALL   FULL, ANNUAL INFLATION ADJUSTEMENT

CHART A12-1

Moderate Balanced Portfolio
Maximun Perpetual "Real" Retirement Income

Initial Portfolio: $1,000,000   Initial Income: $44,000 (4.4% of Original Portfolio)

	The Numbers You See				The Numbers You Feel	
Year	The Portfolio Grows in Nominal $ Even After Paying Out Retiree Distributions	Retiree's Annual Distributions — Increasing Annually with the Full Change in Inflation	CPI: Annual Inflation Rate %	CPI: Cumulative Inflation %	This Portfolio Remains Fairly Stable in Real $ (Adjusted for Inflation)	Retiree's Annual Distributions in Real $ (Adjusted for Inflation)
1972	$1,100,200	$44,000	3.4%	3.4%	$1,063,920	$44,000
1973	1,027,023	47,872	8.8	12.5	912,828	44,000
1974	902,446	53,712	12.2	26.2	714,887	44,000
1975	1,025,639	57,478	7.0	35.1	759,252	44,000
1976	1,118,524	60,242	4.8	41.6	790,013	44,000
1977	1,115,275	64,321	6.8	51.2	737,770	44,000
1978	1,176,302	70,129	9.0	64.8	713,694	44,000
1979	1,297,046	79,463	13.3	86.8	694,513	44,000
1980	1,423,817	89,316	12.4	109.9	678,286	44,000
1981	1,341,751	97,301	8.9	128.7	586,737	44,000
1982	1,505,411	101,067	3.9	137.5	633,777	44,000
1983	1,606,745	104,907	3.8	146.6	651,675	44,000
1984	1,636,517	109,051	4.0	156.3	638,528	44,000
1985	1,987,143	113,162	3.8	166.0	747,166	44,000
1986	2,349,418	114,441	1.1	169.0	873,510	44,000
1987	2,395,329	119,488	4.4	180.8	852,964	44,000
1988	2,568,538	124,769	4.4	193.2	875,927	44,000
1989	2,850,731	130,571	4.7	206.9	928,964	44,000
1990	2,661,154	138,549	6.1	225.6	817,253	44,000
1991	3,007,219	142,789	3.1	235.6	896,110	44,000
1992	2,971,256	146,930	2.9	245.3	860,440	44,000
1993	3,238,638	150,970	2.8	254.8	912,770	44,000
1994	3,095,944	155,001	2.7	264.3	849,862	44,000
1995	3,548,145	158,938	2.5	273.5	949,869	44,000
1996	3,719,585	164,215	3.3	285.9	963,767	44,000
1997	4,005,996	167,007	1.7	292.5	1,020,627	44,000
1998	4,343,860	169,695	1.6	298.8	1,089,171	44,000
1999	4,638,754	174,243	2.7	309.5	1,132,755	44,000
2000	4,514,269	180,150	3.4	323.4	1,066,211	44,000
2001	4,222,082	182,942	1.6	330.0	981,980	44,000
2002	3,941,900	187,296	2.4	340.2	895,502	44,000
2003	4,496,889	190,818	1.9	348.5	1,002,730	44,000
2004	4,728,854	197,038	3.3	363.1	1,021,165	44,000
2005	4,836,709	203,777	3.4	378.9	1,009,916	44,000
2006	5,253,143	208,953	2.5	391.1	1,069,698	44,000
2007	5,527,359	217,478	4.1	411.1	1,081,415	44,000
2008	4,501,032	217,674	0.1	411.6	879,825	44,000
2009	5,086,724	223,595	2.7	425.5	967,982	44,000
2010	5,449,326	226,948	1.5	433.4	1,021,658	44,000
2011	$5,330,641	$233,666	3.0%	449.2%	$970,675	$44,000

PERPETUAL INCOME   FULL, ANNUAL INFLATION ADJUSTEMENT

CHART A12-2

Moderate Balanced Portfolio
Maximun 40-Year "Real" Retirement Income
Initial Portfolio: $1,000,000   Initial Income: $65,000 (6.5% of Original Portfolio)

	The Numbers You See				The Numbers You Feel	
Year	The Portfolio is Deleted After 40 Years of Paying Increasing Retiree Distributions	Retiree's Annual Distributions — Increasing Annually with the 2/3 Change in Inflation	2/3 x CPI: Two-Thirds Annual Inflation Rate %	2/3 x CPI: Two-Thirds Cumulative Inflation%	The Real Value of this Portfolio is Fairly Stable at First —then Declines Steadily	Retiree's Annual Distributions in Real $ (Adjusted for 2/3 Inflation)
1972	$1,079,200	$65,000	2.3%	2.3%	$1,055,212	$65,000
1973	985,565	68,813	5.9	8.3	910,256	63,500
1974	843,151	74,410	8.1	17.1	720,152	59,800
1975	934,062	77,888	4.7	22.6	762,182	54,900
1976	993,132	80,385	3.2	26.5	785,203	52,400
1977	963,344	84,013	4.5	32.2	728,760	50,700
1978	987,563	89,071	6.0	40.1	704,661	48,400
1979	1,058,672	96,974	8.9	52.6	693,833	45,500
1980	1,130,055	104,991	8.3	65.2	684,067	41,400
1981	1,030,898	111,248	6.0	75.0	588,943	38,000
1982	1,120,176	114,119	2.6	79.6	623,851	35,800
1983	1,156,631	117,010	2.5	84.1	628,238	34,800
1984	1,136,473	120,091	2.6	89.0	601,451	34,000
1985	1,335,440	123,109	2.5	93.7	689,422	33,100
1986	1,531,775	124,037	0.8	95.2	784,867	32,200
1987	1,511,929	127,683	2.9	100.9	752,573	32,000
1988	1,568,567	131,446	2.9	106.8	758,417	31,000
1989	1,685,116	135,520	3.1	113.2	790,271	30,100
1990	1,513,912	141,041	4.1	121.9	682,193	29,200
1991	1,648,099	143,918	2.0	126.4	727,813	28,000
1992	1,562,214	146,700	1.9	130.8	676,800	27,400
1993	1,632,784	149,390	1.8	135.1	694,638	26,900
1994	1,486,939	152,049	1.8	139.2	621,528	26,400
1995	1,625,838	154,624	1.7	143.3	668,270	25,900
1996	1,621,596	158,046	2.2	148.7	652,094	25,500
1997	1,659,431	159,837	1.1	151.5	659,831	24,900
1998	1,708,129	161,553	1.1	154.2	671,981	24,700
1999	1,728,167	164,439	1.8	158.7	667,931	24,400
2000	1,580,750	168,155	2.3	164.6	597,452	24,000
2001	1,372,603	169,893	1.0	167.3	513,476	23,400
2002	1,169,817	172,589	1.6	171.6	430,781	23,200
2003	1,216,394	174,752	1.3	175.0	442,388	22,800
2004	1,153,888	178,550	2.2	180.9	410,729	22,500
2005	1,047,309	182,621	2.3	187.3	364,482	22,000
2006	997,013	185,713	1.7	192.2	341,200	21,500
2007	899,569	190,764	2.7	200.2	299,701	21,200
2008	577,083	190,879	0.1	200.3	192,146	20,600
2009	486,502	194,340	1.8	205.8	159,101	20,600
2010	346,604	196,284	1.0	208.8	112,228	20,200
2011	$153,761	$200,157	2.0%	214.9%	$48,823	$20,000

SPEND-IT-ALL   TWO-THIRD, ANNUAL INFLATION ADJUSTEMENT

CHART A12-3

Moderate Balanced Portfolio — Worst Case Study* (Retire in 1968)

Maximun 40-Year "Real" Retirement Income

Initial Portfolio: $1,000,000   Initial Income: $57,000 (5.7% of Original Portfolio)

	The Numbers You See				The Numbers You Feel	
Year	The Portfolio is Depleted After 43 Years of Paying Increasing Retiree Distributions	Retiree's Annual Distributions — Increasing Annually with the 2/3 Change in Inflation	2/3 x CPI: Two-Thirds of Annual Inflation Rate %	2/3 x CPI: Two-Thirds of Cumulative Inflation %	The Real Value of this Portfolio is Fairly Stable at First — then Declines Steadily	Retiree's Annual Distributions in Real $ (Adjusted for 2/3 Inflation)
1968	$1,059,000	$57,000	3.1%	3.1%	$1,026,826	$57,000
1969	930,847	59,318	4.1	7.3	867,297	55,200
1970	939,168	61,493	3.7	11.3	844,099	53,000
1971	994,616	62,887	2.3	13.8	874,121	51,000
1972	1,073,723	64,316	2.3	16.4	922,669	49,900
1973	980,938	68,090	5.9	23.2	796,225	48,700
1974	839,625	73,628	8.1	33.2	630,261	45,900
1975	930,650	77,069	4.7	39.4	667,398	42,100
1976	990,056	79,540	3.2	43.9	687,940	40,200
1977	960,983	83,130	4.5	50.4	638,903	38,900
1978	985,861	88,134	6.0	59.5	618,226	37,100
1979	1,057,700	95,955	8.9	73.6	609,217	34,900
1980	1,130,025	103,887	8.3	88.0	601,179	31,800
1981	1,032,038	110,079	6.0	99.2	518,166	29,200
1982	1,122,741	112,919	2.6	104.3	549,528	27,400
1983	1,160,777	115,779	2.5	109.5	554,108	26,700
1984	1,142,240	118,828	2.6	115.0	531,269	26,000
1985	1,344,137	121,815	2.5	120.4	609,846	25,400
1986	1,543,863	122,732	0.8	122.1	695,226	24,700
1987	1,526,210	126,341	2.9	128.6	667,648	24,500
1988	1,586,008	130,063	2.9	135.3	673,948	23,800
1989	1,706,784	134,095	3.1	142.6	703,462	23,100
1990	1,536,675	139,557	4.1	152.5	608,562	22,400
1991	1,676,557	142,404	2.0	157.7	650,685	21,500
1992	1,593,265	145,158	1.9	162.6	606,630	21,000
1993	1,669,778	147,819	1.8	167.5	624,316	20,600
1994	1,525,673	150,450	1.8	172.2	560,461	20,300
1995	1,673,843	152,998	1.7	176.8	604,653	19,900
1996	1,675,805	156,384	2.2	183.0	592,253	19,600
1997	1,721,929	158,156	1.1	186.2	601,734	19,100
1998	1,780,243	159,854	1.1	189.2	615,506	18,900
1999	1,809,800	162,710	1.8	194.4	614,741	18,700
2000	1,665,130	166,387	2.3	201.1	553,101	18,400
2001	1,456,728	168,106	1.0	204.2	478,927	18,000
2002	1,253,906	170,774	1.6	209.0	405,807	17,800
2003	1,318,231	172,914	1.3	212.9	421,344	17,500
2004	1,267,318	176,672	2.2	219.7	396,454	17,300
2005	1,170,134	180,700	2.3	227.0	357,892	16,900
2006	1,137,672	183,760	1.7	232.5	342,170	16,500
2007	1,055,399	188,758	2.7	241.5	309,020	16,200
2008	712,123	188,872	0.1	241.7	208,384	15,800
2009	647,866	192,297	1.8	247.9	186,204	15,800
2010	528,734	194,219	1.0	251.4	150,460	15,500
2011	$341,838**	$198,052	2.0%	258.3%	$95,393	$15,300

*1968 was the worst possible year to retire in the Inflation Era (1960-1996). This was the kick-off year for the Super Bowl, the huge 14-year bout of inflation, and (not coincidentally) the worst stock market conditions since the Great Depression (1968-1974).
** Minimum of two years's income remaining
Note: Returns provided prior to 1972 represent Domestic Moderate Balanced Model performance. Please refer to The Sure Road to Investment Success, Chapter 10, page 139 for additional information.

SPEND-IT-ALL   TWO-THIRD, ANNUAL INFLATION ADJUSTMENT

CHART A12-4

Bibliography

Bernstein, Peter L. *Against the Gods, The Remarkable Story of Risk*. New York: John Wiley & Sons, 1996.

Bogle, John C. *Bogle on Mutual Funds: New Perspectives for the Intelligent Investor*. New York: Irwin Professional Publishing, 1994.

Bryan, Lowell and Farrell, Diana. *Market Unbound: Unleashing Global Capitalism*. New York: John Wiley & Sons, 1996.

Dimson, Marsh and Staunton, *Triumph of the Optimists* (101 years of Global Investment Returns), Princeton: Princeton University Press, 2002.

Ellis, Charles D. *Investment Policy: How to Win the Loser's Game*. Homewood, Illinois: Business One Irwin, 1985.

Ellis, Charles D. and Vertin, James R. *Classics II: Another Investor's Anthology*. Homewood, Illinois: Dow Jones-Irwin, 1989

Ellis, Charles D. and Vertin, James R. *Classics: An Investor's Anthology*. Homewood, Illinois: Dow Jones-Irwin, 1989

Fisher, Kenneth L. *The Wall Street Waltz*. Chicago: Contemporary Books, Inc., 1987.

Galbraith, John Kenneth. *The Great Crash 1929*. Boston, Massachusetts: Houghton Miffin Co., 1954.

Gibson, Roger C. *Asset Allocation*. Homewood, Illinois: Business One Irwin, 1990.

Graham, Benjamin. *The Intelligent Investor*. New York: Harper & Row, 1973.

Hagstrom, Robert G., Jr. *The Warren Buffett Way*. New York: John Wiley & Sons, 1994.

Hoff, Benjamin. *The Tao of Pooh*. New York: Penguin Books, 1982.

Ibbotson Associates. *Stocks, Bonds, Bills & Inflation 2012 Yearbook*. Chicago, Illinois: Ibbotson Associates, 2012.

Ibbotson, Roger G. and Brinson, Gary P. *Global Investing*. New York: McGraw-Hill, Inc., 1993.

Kotlikoff, Laurence J. & Burns, Scott. *The Clash of Generations*. London, England: The MIT Press, 2012

Lederman, Jess and Klein, Robert A. (Editors). *Global Asset Allocation*. New York: John Wiley & Sons, 1994.

Leuthold, Steven C. *The Myths of Inflation and Investing.* Chicago: Crain Books, 1980.

Lynch, Peter. *Beating the Street.* New York: Simon & Schuster, 1993.

Malkiel, Burton G. *A Random Walk Down Wall Street.* New York: W. W. Norton, 1973, rev. 1991.

O'Higgins, Michael. *Beating the Dow.* New York: Harper-Perennial, 1992.

O'Shaughnessy, James P. *What Works On Wall Street.* New York: McGraw-Hill, Inc., 1997.

Reinhart, Carmen M. & Rogoff, Kenneth S. *This Time Is Different.* New Jersey: Princeton University Press, 2009.

Rosenberg, Claude N., Jr. *Investing with the Best.* New York and Toronto: John Wiley & Sons, 1986.

Siegel, Jeremy J. *Stocks for the Long Run.* Burr Ridge, Illinois: Irwin Professional Publishing, 2008.

The Vanguard Retirement Investing Guide. Chicago: Irwin Professional Publishing, 2001.

Tobias, Andrew. *The Only Investment Guide You'll Ever Need.* San Diego: Harcourt Brace & Co., 1978, rev. 1996.

Train, John. *The Money Masters.* New York: Harper & Row, 1985.

Train, John. *The New Money Masters.* New York: Harper & Row, 1989.

Index